THE SECRETS AND MYSTERIES OF HAWAII

Planetary Crossroads and a Key to Our Future

THE SECRETS AND MYSTERIES OF HAWAII

A CALL TO THE SOUL

With Special Focus on the Big Island
and the Master Key: Madame Pele

PILA OF HAWAII

Health Communications, Inc.
Deerfield Beach, Florida

www.hcibooks.com

Library of Congress Cataloging-in-Publication Data

Pila of Hawaii, (date)
    The secrets & mysteries of Hawaii : a call to the soul /
Pila of Hawaii.
        p. cm.
    ISBN-13: 978-1-55874-362-5 (trade paper)
    ISBN-10: 1-55874-362-6 (trade paper)
    1. Kahuna—Hawaii. 2. Spiritual healing—Hawaii.
    3. Legends—Hawaii. 4. Mythology, Hawaiian.
    5. Hawaii—Religious life and customs. I. Title.
    BL2630.H38P55 1995
    299'.92—dc20   95-25538
                                                              CIP

HCI, its logos, and marks are trademarks of
Health Communications, Inc.

Publisher: Health Communications, Inc.
            3201 S.W. 15th Street
            Deerfield Beach, Florida 33442-8190

R-11-11

Author may be contacted at his website: www.MysticalHawaii.com

# Dedication

To David "Papa" Bray, son of the great *kahuna*, Daddy Bray. Daddy knew what he was doing when you received his dying breath in the amulet, David. You have shown and lived the real power beyond the tricks of the trade. Anyone who has ever witnessed the sweetness of your blessings knows your spirit. The tradition of those who would carry the banner and the crest is shifting from the eldest and the macho to the one who has the real courage beyond the armor. The one who dares to be vulnerable enough to show heart.

Power trips are no longer allowed on our planet at this critical time in her evolution. From here on there shall be swift and severe consequences. This is what has caused the karmic genocide of all peoples throughout time. As we reach critical mass at this defining moment in all history, we as a race are beginning to sense that the future is not totally new. Here, in the islands that our world knows as Paradise, the indigenous tribes of the world are finding that their roots are the same. Legend tells of a time before history when these islands were the tips of a continent called *Mu*. With a dimension beyond the written word, ancient chants speak of a star from whence we came. This legend is now coming full circle. As blood denounces blood and tribe fights tribe in power struggles that only put more nails into their coffins, the true *mana* still returns, the *mana loa*.

In the twilight of your passing, know that you were the chosen one, David. In my healings with you I had intuited the past. The misspent youth, the abuse, all the while trying to live up to your father's concept of Man. Still, despite it all, your sweetness has shown through. May this be what you are remembered for by all your family, students and friends. Your spirit, like the spirit of the ancestors, lives forever in the hearts that you have touched who will reach the hearts of others. Beyond the bloodline called *Ali i* (royal) this is the higher meaning of passing on the lineage. It was from this place of love that I made my commitment to you and the Hawaiian People. For here is the only power that can heal an entire planet in her time of most desperate need. The full meaning and understanding of that power has been captured in one word only once. In all the languages of the Earth, that word is *aloha. Aloha nui loa,* David. *Meke mahalo.*

To Those of Hawaiian Ancestry:

This is my *mana'o*. I have no *kumu*. About the controversy over "the old ways" I must clarify this. A Hawaiian recently told me, "I wish I knew about the wisdom of the *kahunas*. My grandfather refused to tell me anything because of the "curse." Now there is a generation of children not speaking Hawaiian who are, for all practical purposes, disconnected from their heritage. This must change. Na'ope and a few other "special ones" with a great deal of courage and diplomacy, have brought back the dance. With few exceptions the rest of the old ways remain *kapu. kahunas* of the dark claiming power do not have it. They play the games of fear and pain that cost you everything. Others of you, the true *kahunas,* who still hold the thread of knowing, wait quietly.

This work is dedicated to the *Ancient Tradition* as a tribute to the self-worth of the Hawaiian people. From my humble viewpoint yours is the most important teaching and way of life that can be shared with a planet in her time of crisis.

I do not claim to know it all and I am not a learned man. Quite the opposite. Until a few years ago I was dyslexic and could not read without great difficulty. Instead of continuing college I ended up in a rice paddy, which led to a straight jacket. Since my near-death experiences in the combat of Vietnam I have "seen" certain things about the future and the past. Things about the Big Island and her sisters. Things about the Hawaiian culture, particularly about the time before *kapu,* which I refer to as "the Ancient Way". Others have also begun to refer to the original teaching in this manner. Legend speaks of its return.

I am not another self-proclaimed *kahuna* and do not call myself one. I am not a haoli either and less than a half-breed, but I believe it is my Cherokee blood that has called me home. The home I have been looking for and have never known on Earth. *Kahuna* is a title I believe should be reserved for the Hawaiian people to declare, as the pride and dignity of the old ways returns. By the turn of the century this title will mean more than Ph.D. To me it will always mean more than any of the titles that men bestow upon men. All I want to be called is your friend. To someday be called brother would be the highest honor I could know and the real welcome home.

At the threshold of any time of change, it is necessary to survival to clarify the sociological belief systems. This determines the health and very sanity of a culture. No matter what the individual beliefs are, we are all influenced in this manner. Since this is the time of greatest change in all history and survival of the planet is in the balance, all her citizens must take a cold hard look at this belief system, which forms our foundation for living. We must glean what is true before going on, leaving behind what is no longer valid. A time of change doesn't invalidate everything. Indeed, the so-called "new age" may not be new at all. There is something strangely familiar coming out of all the strange and radical trends upon us. For those seekers looking for answers I offer that "A Key to the Future lies in the Past." For you, the Hawaiians, I offer that the answers lie in the blood. *Ali'i* is not what you think it is; take it from a half-breed who has lived the betrayal of the only war in history where there were no heroes. The royalty you seek is not in the lineage passed down by man. It is within you and your acceptance of your own self-worth. It maybe is easier to remember if you have a drop of Hawaiian blood, for the spiral of the memory is more complete within you.

The time has come to bring your true story to light, for it is shared with "Tribal Peoples" the world over. Their roots are the wisdom you know as *huna*. Since the mid eighties a sojourn has taken place on the Big Island of Hawaii. Shamen returning here from all over the world are finding that the teaching is the same. From the American and Canadian Indian to the Maori and the Aboriginal, their *kahunas/shamans* know and together hold a key, for all Humankind. One that can unlock our future and see through the clouds. A key that can only be turned by the child. One who has put aside childishness. One who has had the courage to embrace innocence again and regain the power, the childlike wonderment.

Come, take another look . . . at a small piece of the most wonderful and powerful teaching in the world. The teaching that was once a way of life for you, the original "stewards of the garden." The garden that the world calls Paradise and the stewards that legend knows as . . . *"the Children of the Rainbow."*

En Memorium

Uncle George *Lanakilakekiahiali'l* Na'ope,
"Hawaii's Living Golden Treasure"
Your legacy lives, and in a time of anger
and chaos, may you shine even brighter.

Sweet Prince, Aloooha,

—Pila

Contents

# Acknowledgments

To my fellow soul traveler,
Claire "Kalar" Chiles, known also to me
in this lifetime as "Mom."

To Mimi, who taught a boy to
believe in magic and gave him a precious
legacy, the thread of a dream and
the reason to hang on.

To Christa, Patti Rose, Jennifer, and
Brian, my joy along the way.

Paradise Found...

There is a place in the heart beyond time that legend calls Paradise.

Cloaked in a mystery that was unattainable, it remained locked away in the fairy realm, like the mythical Brigadoon.

Until her discovery by Western man, Hawaii lay shrouded in the secrecy that comes with being the most remote destination on Earth, unknown to all save her stewards, whom legend has named the "Children of the Rainbow."

Today she still holds the secret, a Crown Mystery, veiled to the physical senses of ordinary man. After all these centuries it lies buried, like a pirate's treasure, waiting to be unearthed.

The Crown Mystery eludes the uninitiated, those minds preoccupied with the trite details of clocks and schedules, just as the billowy clouds of Hawaii were its camouflage for all those centuries; as though an artist's brush had carefully blended the islands of Paradise into the blue that escaped the eyes of man, engulfed in the deeper blue void that is the greatest of oceans.

In a modern world half gone mad, a clue surfaces to unlock the mystery yet for most it remains hidden, not afar in some obscure horizon, but within. It is a piece of a puzzle within a broken spiral of a memory of who we really are and where we came from.

Hidden and yet in plain sight, now sensed, the location near, somewhere between a confusion in the head and a yearning in the heart.

For those who drink of the words, the spiral rebraids, a thought once familiar of a memory that fades. Pieces of puzzles makeup a key, unlocking a clue to set yourself free.

Come pierce the veil, rediscover the key, turn away from the war, the adventure to see.

Remember your friends from a long time ago, around an old campfire, a song for the soul.

The stewards of Paradise beckon you home, to solve the mystery that first caused us to roam.

No path is straight for they all take a bend, to spiral around starting over again.

All things above are like that below, the greater it is the smaller you go.

So quiet your head and follow your heart. The spiral a circle comes back to the start.

A doorway opens that's always been sealed, secrets and mysteries finally revealed.

PART I
Lifting the Veil

*"In the hemisphere where
East meets West, there exists the place
known to all the world as Paradise.
It is the most remote of all
destinations on our planet Earth.
Legend proclaims Hawaii as
The Crossroads Between Worlds.
Today, as all humanity stands
at the crossroads, modern science is
finally beginning to fathom
this ancient connection."*

—Pila of Hawaii,
Opening Address
The New York Theosophical Society,
January, 1995

 # One

Vacation:
The New Dimension

A Sojourn of Rejuvenation
and Discovery

Va.ca'tion: n. 1. A period of release from work; holiday. 2. Act of vacating.

Va'cate": v.t. 1. to make vacant, quit, empty. 2. make void, annul.

So.journ: Adventure of discovery. A quest for knowledge.

> *"In this tidal wave of change upon us, the vacation 'want to get away from' has turned into the 'need to get in touch with.' What sufficed to relax and rejuvenate the body must now encompass the increasingly confused and troubled mind. Until now considered a*

frivolity, the new definition for vacation encompass-
es a need that is vital to the balance of our mental
well being. Our world is in a core level identity crisis
which extends all the way into biblical prophecy. In
the turmoil of reidentifying our very foundation
stones of belief, finding a temporary sanctuary for
the mind may become a matter of survival."

—from *The Tidal Wave of Change:*
Lesson #1, How to Surf
by Pila

As civilization escalates to a turning point and the turn of
a millennium, we find ourselves overworked, overfed, over-
stimulated and overwhelmed. We have entered a new
dimension that we have yet to fathom. Our physical world
of laboring over crops has become a mental world of com-
puterized automation. The time we take to refresh, renew
and relax becomes more and more important. In a world
redefining itself we seem to have lost something. Outdated
concepts of the 1950s vacation no longer satiates the growing hunger of an increasingly unsettled mind. Those who
have the finances to address the need are finding that time
spent dreaming about the vacation is more fulfilling than
actually being there. Something is missing.

Let us look back and see if we can begin to find an
answer or two. Who knows? Perhaps the answer to deeper
questions that plague us as a society may await us also, if
we know where to look.

Let us start with the modern vacation to the most desirous
of all locations on Earth. Recent Gallup polls indicate that
three-quarters of the world, if given a blank check, would
choose Hawaii as their vacation destination, including former communist countries.

The Old Approach

The average vacationer has saved for more than a year. For many it has been a lifetime. If you are a hardworking aspiring executive, business owner or self-made person, see if this sounds familiar:

You have wrenched yourself out of the rat race for a week of solitude in Paradise. You have trucked halfway across the world, schlepping your baggage through three airports, at least two buses and a half-dozen cabs. At your destination you reach a hotel room just like the one you left, except for strange music and hot, thick air. Exhausted and worn out, you turn in the first night, feeling somehow cheated.

This first day is glorious, however, indeed Paradise. You stand on the lanai and take a deeper breath than you have in years. The early morning air is warm, its breeze steady and consistent, reassuring and somehow nurturing. How could you have labeled it as just hot and thick? Azure waves cleanse a perfect beach, gracing a calm bay of clear turquoise and blue, riddled with coral reefs. Palms sway gently in the balmy trade winds, against a backdrop of deep green, crushed velvet, tropical splendor. The surreal colors with their exotic fragrances and air that you can now taste quickly drown into memory your thoughts of an old sterile working world.

Breakfast is served with an orchid on your plate in the perfect outdoor weather. Plain eggs will never be the same again. A bird seemingly dressed for the occasion in a black tuxedo and bright red cap begs for crumbs at your table. Later, after breakfast, you walk barefoot on the beach, rolling up your pant legs to wade. You eyes cannot drink enough. The ink-painted, fluorescent fish of the coral reef bay demand further exploration.

You settle for the affluence of cocktail service and sunbathing poolside. The first day is labeled "jet lag" to quell the ruckus within. The vacation of a lifetime has been salvaged and, to this point everything is perfect.

The second day goes by as equally relaxing. A leisurely stroll in the village is sprinkled with a bit of shopping, reserving the big buys for the wisdom that comes from checking out the territory. In a moment of wild abandon you purchase a ridiculous Hawaiian shirt. With a bravery you didn't know you possessed, you actually wear it out of the store. For a while you glance around in defense of any laughter. No one notices. Others are wearing wild shirts too, in couple look alikes. People pass by in the same one you are wearing, with some wearing outlandish flowers in their hair. You note how absurd it is for men to behave that way.

You have a delightful fresh catch lunch in an open air cafe, seaside. Common food—now has dormant tastebuds exploding in orgasm.

Back at the hotel the sunset is a technicolor celebration, serenaded by native music you have never given a moments notice to before, now exquisite to your ears. Another mai-tai is ordered and paid for by flashing your room key. After all, it is your vacation. You forget that the ingredients are 140 proof. It slams you in the face with a goofy smile. Everything is wonderful to the point of wanting to kiss strangers.

The third day begins early with surprisingly little hangover. This calls for sport and adventure. You decide between snorkeling, a four-wheel drive tour and a half-day cruise. Parasailing, the submarine and the more exotic sports are tabled with insincere thoughts of tomorrow.

There is still good sun when you return. After all that work, its poolside again. Now to work once more on that tan. The thought brings a smile as you beckon the waiter. The office crew back home warned you of how lethal the sun could be at the equator. You have been wise from day one by using a number eight screen. After all, a tan is the only proof of where you have been. It must be captured and worn as a symbol, even though the evidence can only be flaunted in front of co-workers for a week or so.

Then, it begins to creep in. Something causes you to refuse the second drink. The vacation inspired by the opulence of the 1940s and 1950s now has something missing. You don't quite understand. Like planting the first flag on Everest your new territory has been claimed and its sanctuary declared. Here is the quiet you have waited for with no demands and the nothing to do you have looked forward to for ages.

Then, because nature abhors a vacuum, it begins. Two days of the frivolous dreams of owning an island decay, and then they are compromised. Another vacation in six months instead of a year you think, or perhaps next time two weeks instead of just one. Suddenly all thoughts turn to reflection. Like a dam bursting, the whole book of your life's memories flops open and dumps itself into your lap. You feel regrets for time lost and a sense of not getting all you can here and now. The remaining thread of a dream of early retirement is flash-flooded by job insecurity. Things that never concerned you that you can do nothing about now, threaten your peace of mind. The world situation, politics, Social Security and the questionable solvency of your company. The extra mai-tai is reordered. Unknown to you, an invisible clock has begun to tick on an unpronounced sentence. The long-awaited moment in Paradise is now running out. With effort and the fruit-filled glass and its umbrella, the invasion of your mind is all pushed aside. You eat the fruit from two more umbrellas forgetting to add the total number. Everything is copacetic.

The rest of your coveted vacation days become blurred. hours become seconds that run into "Where did the week go?" The final judgment comes down to "Wait another year," as your bags are pushed onto the street by the jailor that used to be your doorman. The executioner awaits you with the enormous front desk bill. You grant yourself a final meal.

It was semi-wonderful. It was Paradise, certainly, with a beauty that just couldn't be captured. In the middle it somehow started to slip through your fingers. What was missing? Somewhere along the line something went wrong. You suspect it happened long ago, before the trip. You just weren't able to connect. Too many worries. Too many other things going on, inside.

The ride to the airport brings in the clouds. Your heart is heavy and you are supposed to be feeling fulfilled. On the plane as the islands drift away into the horizon you think, "A year is a lifetime away."

What Was Missing?

Why doesn't the old getaway work anymore?

How did it come to this? When did it begin and where was the dividing line so that we can get the train back on the track?

And back in the work-a-day world there is a larger question still. When did the fun of competition, which built our incredible world of conveniences, lose itself in the madness of the game and become a separation from spirit? And, more importantly, how do we heal the severed connection? Why is Hawaii, the most remote, get-away-from-it-all destination, so important to reestablishing that connection? Why do you now think only of giving it all up and moving there? And the worst thing is that you know it is only an unrealistic fantasy.

People who have experienced the above scenario recently seem to be reacting in two different ways. Some have tried to drop their entire lives and move to Hawaii to try to connect with what touched their souls when visiting there. Others, out of frustration, look for that connection elsewhere next vacation time. Some cover the feeling up with chemicals or the diversion that is the competitive rat race game. The rest of us work our butts into an early grave dreaming about someday retiring in Paradise. A few are actually happy where they are and that means that, either they have found the keys to happiness or have the I.Q. of a kumquat and will always be satisfied with Budweiser and Monday night football. For those of you still dreaming about retirement, forget about it. The belief of retiring from life is now obsolete and under the full cardiac arrest called our Social Security system. There is no retirement from life. Once we accept that, then we can begin to loosen the death grip we have on other obsolete beliefs, such as old age equals bad health—a conviction which may be the culprit for growing old and dying. Perhaps I can shed some more light on these concepts later on with the wonderful secrets from Paradise that I have to share with you.

Let us start with how it really began for us all, for the human race. Perhaps then, in this most defining moment in all history, we can begin to address something that we may all be looking for deep down. Making sense of it all cannot happen with the masses, but with thinking individuals like you who intuitively pick up little books like this perhaps it can. For you there is a deeper understanding that can be regained in the connection we reach for called Paradise. A connection that can rejuvenate the body, mind and spirit and begin to make sense of a larger picture that is unfolding on our planet at this critical juncture in our time.

The Hawaiian tradition of sharing wisdom comes from storytelling. The old ones, the ancestors, considered all life a symbolic metaphor and contended that the truth may be closer to legend, myth and fairytale than we realize. Because of the creativity inherent in our myths and the heart-felt joy with which we share them with our precious children, it is said that *ano, ano i'o,* (the real seedling of truth) can be found in our legends and fairytales. Truth is the source behind the inspiration of creativity. Whenever you experience joy, in the Hawaiian interpretation, a part of you knows that you are hearing the true voice of God.

There are places in the beautiful islands of Hawaii where one can go to get in touch with things at a deeper level. Hawaii is the perfect stage setting for such connections, if you know what to look for and how to look. That is the purpose of this book. The great thinkers who mold our way of life as well as concerned everyday individuals must now have places to go where they can stand outside of their situations and process. In the time of greatest change I believe this to be Hawaii's destiny. These places within the islands have special energy and are incredibly healing and inspirational. From such a place on the Big Island that I call the "Edge of Eternity," this is the legend of how it all began as it came to me intuitively . . .

 # Two

How We
Lost the Way:
A Hawaiian Legend

Paradise Lost—the
Fall from Grace

Long, long ago, after the density and the separation but
before time was given its meaning, there existed the Kingdom
of LeMuria, held in legend and folklore the world over as Mu.
Hawaiian legend says that their islands of Paradise are the
tips of that continent. If the history called Mankind were an
inch on a yardstick, the time legend knows as Atlantis would
show up as six inches before that, somewhat overlapping the
rest of the measurement, framing LeMuria. Before that was a
land called Pan. Remnants of its legend exist through Greek

Mythology, the legends of King Arthur and Merlin and the great myth bringer, *Walt Disney's, Peter, the Pan*. Although the creature spirits of Pan prevailed and intermingled with the culture of LeMuria, it is the latter that is the interest of this work. People then had the constant spirit connection with the God force of the Universe, a "God-Link"™ that has eluded Humankind since. They described this relationship accurately by naming themselves, the *Children* of God's promise, *the Rainbow*. The God-force that permeated all life was called *huna,* the invisible life essence. Stewards of this force were called *kahunas,* ambassadors of the essence.

This time before time was a Heaven on Earth. The children of the most high God lived as though immortal without concern or disease.

Once upon that time . . . in fact when time was given its meaning, the *Children of the Rainbow* began to lose their connection. It happened one day around sunset while they were playing one of the games of life.

No one really knows how it happened, only that it had to do with taking the game too seriously. For a while the Children had used a silly concept called darkness in an effort to contrast the boundaries of their joy, which was limitless before that time.

This came after the notion of an angry storm but far before the sillier notion of "good guys and bad guys." The only actual offense committed by the Children was in forgetting that it was a game to begin with and therein began the serious and far-reaching consequences.

Still being Children playing games, they were unaware of the disastrous effects that could result in crossing a small thin line. A line that separated innocence from ignorance.

Several other things happened during this time of game playing. Certain of these Children, because of their aptitudes, were made stewards of pieces of their wisdom.

In a forgetful mood—no one quite remembered why—
one such *kahuna* child one day withheld his wisdom when
it was needed. Others emulated this silly game as Children
are known to do, like little monkeys. Finding the game distasteful the rest of the Children ignored them, unaware that
this ignorance was still a form of playing the game.

No one realized that the brilliant Rainbow above their
heads had begun to fade.

Proportionately a strange and eerie feeling began to seed
itself in their little tummies, just below the navel.

No one noticed the passion dwindling in their game-playing.

The Rainbow was the most beautiful phenomenon in their
garden playground. Bridging the two basic play worlds, its
brilliance was more real than anything in their denser reality.

The Rainbow was also dependable and normally followed the Children through each twilight and into the night.
They were curious, as all children are, and always explor-
ing the endless variety of life. They very much enjoyed the
game called learning, from the great library they knew as
their Earth Mother. Perhaps this is why the Rainbow was
taken for granted, even though it was the most vivid of
their realities.

The Rainbow was at the center of all their earlier games.
Its substance could be physically traveled upon to other
worlds and dimensions. The Rainbow inverted itself at night
into a mirror, which was the source of wonderment and
magic and the time the Children looked forward to most of
all. In its mirror the children were able to dance and play
with all their ancestors, feeling the reassurance of departed
loved ones and hearing their wonderful stories and legends.
Here, in the wonder of magical nightfall, the games of the
day were cleansed away so that fresh ones could be started
anew on the morrow.

The night was created for this "mirroring," for strengthening their connection and for remembering. It also served to contrast and complement the sometimes blinding daylight. Through the night they would feel the deeper love of their ancestors and their Maker and rest in the comfort of immortality. The night always brought trust.

Then one night something was different. The Children knew it. It had started earlier that day during one of their games. It was the first time they paid any attention to that funny, uncomfortable feeling inside. They still eagerly awaited the god/goddess *Laka Hina* to usher in the Night Rainbow, but something wasn't right.

In the eleventh hour a murmur rippled through the crowd of little upturned faces. Deep swallows produced a moment of silence and the funny feeling flooded their being, defining itself as something that they had never felt before: fear.

It was almost unbearable. Desperately they cuddled together, searching the skies. *Laka Hina,* the Moon Goddess, made her sojourn across the sky in silence. But this time there was no rainbow. The connection had been severed. The unbearable fear engulfed them, plagued by their moans of sadness. The sounds of their own moans rippled throughout the desperate gathering. They survived the night until morning, realizing somehow they had caused what had happened.

For the first time they felt bad.

The crisp morning air was permeated with an icy silence. It echoed as shudders throughout their being and almost to the bottom of their souls as something that had never haunted them before. From then on, this feeling was known as *abandonment.*

That day a new game began in Paradise based upon the fear of the coming nightfall. For the first time many Children were out sick. The rumor was stomach problems. The rest of the Children, except for a few, showed up with their tummy aches and played at the game anyway, but this time with a new role—victim.

Some *kahunas,* the ones who had created the problem by becoming too full of self, pretended something else and played a different game this time. Feeling bad about what they had done, they pretended to hide their fear and acted as though they still had the connection that had been lost.

Maybe it was a noble gesture and maybe not. They had met before the games and whispered at the far edge of the garden. They surmised that their playmates were hurting and it had always been their responsibility to help. Besides, what they had done didn't warrant all the ruckus and concern. After all, they were only innocent children, or so they told each other. This would have been all right except for one thing—they had lied.

Legend speaks of this gathering at the edge of the garden as the moment that the severing was irreconcilable and set in stone. It is said that the first club was formed at this meeting. They named the club "Better Than the Others" and the word "secret" took on a permanent new meaning. Before this time of separation, the game word "secret" was used to surprise and delight. It is here where it became the tool of destruction used for manipulation and control that would erode all attempts to heal the severed connection. The meeting at the edge of the garden was marked by a little black cloud which continued to hover over every such meeting thereafter—a black cloud that could be felt but seldom seen.

Games continued to grow in lies and distortion as fear and separation snowballed and grew larger each night.

As they played the eerie new game based on withholding information, the *kahunas* began to notice within themselves a strange remnant of the ecstasy which was once their connection. It wasn't the same, they agreed in whispers at the edge of the garden, but it was something, and it was all that was left.

The cloud above their meetings grew darker and more sinister each morning as they met to control the games of the day.

This ghost of ecstasy within the *kahunas* would increase every time one of their playmates, thinking that the *kahuna* still had the connection, would ask for help. The feeling increased further when they discovered that they could force their playmates to do things. They called that feeling power . . . but it wasn't. It was the opposite.

Because of the severed connection, the feeling of power became like a drug exciting the dark *kahunas* in sexual lust instead of love. The addiction grew. The helpless became enslaved. Then the power-hungry began to fight among themselves. An old game-word that used to be harmless became infected with new meaning. That word was "competition."

One night, while most of the children were waiting in agony for the dawn to drown themselves once more in the game, a new word was formed out of the desperation and fear of separation. Fostered by the drug power in the fighting and misery of the night this most dreaded of all words came into being.

That word was "murder."

In the morning the rest of the children banded together and rioted, casting the power-hungry children and most of the *kahunas* out of the Garden. Other words were formed amid the turmoil and based upon the obscene. The greatest of these went unnoticed at first. It would become known throughout time as the perpetrator of wars and misery and the falsehoods of God. Contracted from fear and layered in denial, the word became known later as "self-righteousness."

And so, with deep sadness, the offenders and suspects were all cast upon the water in small boats that had been made in their earlier game-playing. Some of the big black children and the red-haired, green- and blue-eyed ones willingly left with great courage on a quest to find the lost connection. The red-haired, green- and blue-eyes looked to the seven sister stars for guidance. The blacks looked to the Earth and horizon.

All were cast in several directions to *Tahiti,* which then meant "alone or away from." They left in a flood of tears, as gut wrenching as their first night of knowing abandonment, taking with them pieces of the wisdom. Although the key remained with those who stayed, the original teaching split into three factions. Around the world they would later be known as three orders of wisdom. They were later called the *Essenes* or the sensitives, the *Maggi* who were the magicians, and the *Therapeuti,* who were the thinkers, intellectuals and problem solvers.

A time of numbness and complacency followed in Paradise, which then became *the* new definition for *peace* and *quiet.* Then a huge storm hit, followed by great earthquakes. The entire continent of their garden home began to sink into the ocean. The remaining children washed up on the shores of now separate islands, the mountain tops that were once their beloved continent of *Mu.*

Storms had happened whenever the bad new words were used, but nothing had ever happened to this magnitude. They survived, thinking that it was the act of an angry God for what their brothers and sisters had done.

The children, too wrapped up in the fear of surviving these storms, had never connected them with the power of the words that were the denial of their own life-force. They didn't realize their connection in helping to cause the storms, let alone the great earthquakes. They forgot that when they had *peace of mind* it was connected to *peace in the garden.* That knowledge had been severed also. When they realized they had been spared, they found they were able to travel back and forth between the tops of the mountains that remained of their beautiful Garden. Faith became the memory of the connection to God, who became more and more unknowable. A question formed in the place where the connection once stood within them. Was the loving God they once knew now a God of anger?

Since the time when the connection had been severed there were only pale rainbows in what remained of Paradise. They existed almost like memories and could no longer be touched. In fact they ran away every time the children tried to ride them.

Before the separation there was only one rule to live by in Paradise. That rule was to treat others as you would like to have yourself be treated.

Because of the despicable new word, murder, a different set of rules was instilled, all of them based upon denial.

From that day, the Children began to describe their entire world in untruths. They began to base their guidelines for living and playing on what they no longer wanted. Typhoons, hurricanes and earthquakes became commonplace. The legend says that then grew the roots of the kapu system, which means "the rules of the forbidden." They thought they were correcting what had happened so it wouldn't happen again. In reality they had begun playing the same game of separation that they had blamed on the other outcast children.

A wall of fear crept slowly in and around their remaining moments of Joy, enveloping them from underneath. They began, for the first time, to age and die. As solace for their sadness, they continued their games, but with an added element—drudgery. For almost an eternity, Joy became buried as play turned into work. For the outcasts work had already turned into survival. The memory of Joy, like the Rainbow, faded until nothing was left except a glimmer, locked away in the legends and fairytales of what was. This most power-ful of all words, "Joy," which was the connection itself, became shackled by another new and sad word called "Hope." Instead of at the beginning of all games, Joy was then placed at the end as a reward for Drudgery and then finally at the end of their lives. This most prized divine birthright was then labeled a goal to be someday attained through misery. The word "Being" was discarded and replaced with another new word, "Becoming." Joy was rarely ever even glimpsed from that time on. Because of what had happened the physical expression of Joy known as Ecstacy was pushed down into denial. Ecstacy was the fountain of creativity within the Children. It was the current of their link with God, their God-Link. Their denial pushed it physically down just below their little navels and com-pressed it into guilt. The games became meaningless and their bodies atrophied somewhat, unable to conduct the full current of their God-Link™ any longer. Out of this time came the order of the god *Lono,* as a means for survival. It was an order of cold logic where all warmth and compas-sion was forbidden because of the fear of feeling. From this another legend was born that someday Joy would return and the connection would be healed. The severing was now permanent for centuries—to be sealed in guilt. The memory of it was born as a broken spiral in future generations.

For centuries and centuries there was nothing much to do but weather storms and labor to produce the food that the storms had ruined. It was not fun and what was left of Paradise became a prison of "doing time" as life ticked away. Still, in all, it was the closest thing to Paradise on Earth. Unknown to the Children of the Rainbow, around the world their lost brothers and sisters were still alive. Boredom for them had been replaced with the games of conquer, survival and the eternal quest to regain the severed connection.

Then one day in Paradise, a boy on scout duty, high on a cliff, spotted something on the western horizon. The sound of the conch shell rippling over the villages brought mixed feelings of terror and excitement. It was an unsettling feeling for the Children, but it was great to feel alive again.

A small envoy from the biggest boat they had ever seen came ashore, led by a tall, ominous figure dressed in white. He called himself *Pa'ao*. He pointed to a star that he said he was named after and insinuated that his birthname had to do with greatness. Rumors spread of the great ghost who wore the color of death. Other rumors questioned why he would name himself after that particular star. When rumors spoke of the other meaning for his name having to do with clouds and the underworld, they were stifled as being impolite. He was the first adult that the Children, even the old and wrinkled ones, had ever met. He acted friendly enough, so it seemed, and asked many questions with a thick, hard accent. Because of their giving nature and their longing, the Children welcomed him wherever he went. But something just wasn't right.

Through the centuries, as the Children of the Rainbow had spread out to all the peaks of *Mu*, called Hawai'i, each tribe had adopted a color of their beloved rainbow as its own. Each color reflected the nature, weather and energy of their island and their relationship with it. They did this specifically to cherish each band or frequency of the color until the time came that legend said the lost connection to the Rainbow and God would return.

Mixing all physical colors together, one tribe prided themselves on wearing black. They liked the excitement of the elements and nested on the stormy windward side of their island, claiming to be closest to the connection and the returning. In an effort to heal their great loss, they liked to think themselves more powerful. But the legends that they created remained only in their minds. The others considered them frisky and humored them in the creativity of their game. Accents had become noticeable with the different tribes, and theirs was the thickest.

This black-clothed tribe was the most upset by seeing the tall visitor dressed in white.

After the strange visitor departed, stories about him spread from campfire to campfire. Since many had actually touched him and survived, the ghost stories helped them through their now dark and endless nights.

Still, most of the stories were not nice.

Prevalent in the stories was the fact that the man in white had avoided eye contact. Those who held his gaze, said there was something hauntingly familiar and sinister about it. His shallow, stern little, beady eyes masked a deep hurt, said the chieftess of the purple tribe. Never before had they beheld eyes without warmth. It was an important factor that could not be overlooked. It curdled their blood, kindling ghost stories around the campfire for years. This added excitement to the long days that now existed in Paradise. The occasional visits back and forth increased between the brothers and sisters of each island, bringing back a little variety to the boredom that Paradise had become.

One day, the conch sounded again. Then other conches sounded continually. The Children rushed to every shore to behold a spectacle as never seen before. The entire horizon was blood red with painted boats. A wave of fear carried the message throughout the islands. As the armada approached a larger boat was seen leading the rest.

Standing tall on the bow was the Great Ghost of all their stories. Big warriors stormed the shore furiously attacking the Children. Sheer panic swept over them as all their fears and terror suddenly possessed them, magnetizing this horrible event. The last remnant of their innocence was butchered, as a river of blood soaked all the beaches. The most horrible of all words that had not been spoken for centuries begat another word—"war." Although totally defenseless now, the Children of Paradise fought back, to no avail. The horrible word spread throughout all the islands except one.

When these ruthless warriors tried to attack the Island of *Moloka'i* they were met on the shore by the smallest of the tribes called the *Manahuna*. Of all the tribes throughout the mountain peaks of *Mu*, they had remained closest to what had been. Because of the heart connection of their island, they had remembered something that the others had forgotten. Perhaps it was in the childlike reverence that had remained in the remnants of their games. Perhaps it was because in the despair of their loss they had let go of anger. Or perhaps it was because they could still hear the distant echo from the place within. The place next to the breath, the quiet place between heartbeats where their legends said the severing had occurred. Nevertheless, they were already waiting when the warriors arrived.

Three times the sea was filled with the red assault upon the island *Moloka'i*. Three times the assault failed. Legends since that time from the mighty warriors say that the Manahunas were quietly singing when they stormed the beaches. It is said that the tone of their songs caused the warriors' angry spears to arch, miss their mark and fall short.

When the warriors charged forward with their bodies it is said that the song grew louder and the warriors lost their breath, grasped their throats and fell to their knees.

In those nights, in the midst of all the horrible bloodshed, more legends were formed around the campfires— legends of the little people and the magic of the island never-conquered.

After this devastating slaughter and enslavement on the

rest of the islands, the Great White Ghost installed the forbidden system of rules called *kapu*, calling himself the edict of god and adding many more rules, all of them punishable by death.

His story, from then on known as the word "history," began covering up the rest of the truths that existed since the severing and separation. Some of the magic remained, most of it black. None of it had near the power it once possessed.

The Ghost created a royal bloodline based upon *Ku*, known from that day forward as the Angry Warrior God. *Manna*, or power, was then based upon male domination and size.

Things got worse.

At the height of their frenzied addiction to power the returned *kahunas* began to sacrifice their own kind. They attempted this first as a last-ditch effort to re-establish the lost connection. They called this the supreme sacrifice. Then it took on sexual overtones and eventually manifested as a total defiance of the most high father-mother God of love.

Human sacrifice was the crudest and most despicable display of all the effects of the drug called power. All the while this was going on the others turned their heads. They had forgotten that this was a form of permission and participation in the slaughter of innocents. Feeling powerless to do anything, they now felt a strange security in being dominated. Surely this security was the trust that they felt in the nights before the separation. Centuries of forgetfulness had buried their ability to realize that their silence was a surrendering of their own real power and a support for these unspeakable acts. As a result, future generations were born with the guilt of these acts in their cellular memory.

A future holocaust beyond all the horrors they had ever experienced was then cast in stone. Throughout history others called this *karma*.

One day, in a recent century, amid the warring games, a strange craft carrying strange people arrived on the horizon. They knew this would happen. The *kahunas* could still see a little of the future through the blur of the fading legends of their ancestors. What they didn't see in the remnant left of their psychic abilities was that there was a time coming when their entire race would witness the loss of everything. The land, what was left of their religion and two out of three of all their loved ones would die slowly and miserably before them. They would be *ignorant* of any knowledge of why God would allow this to happen. They would not know that the same thing was happening to their lost brothers and sisters who had not returned. Around the world they could be identified as the "tribal peoples," those who remained close to the Earth and had not aspired technologically.

And so, they greeted the strangers and their magnificent ships. There was no memory left of these brothers and sisters, as their lineage had been mixed and diluted through the centuries. The strangers had taken another path, and had been gone too long from Paradise to remember in the spiral of their cells any real connection. Only one legend was left of their origins in Paradise. An incomplete story that once called them the adventurers and told of the color of their hair, skin and eyes and the star they came from. Because of their lost connection the strangers to Paradise were interested in only one thing—ownership. By the time the Hawaiians realized they still had the greater power it was too late. They had assumed the strange white leader who called himself Cook, was their god of legend, *Lono.* He was killed when they realized their mistake.

Others of Cook's kind arrived, proclaiming that all of the Children were born in sin. They preached of an angry God and called them heathens and savages because of the lack of shame about their bodies and their sexuality. Their children were taught to close their eyes and beg for forgiveness and cover their shameful bodies. With their self-worth in shambles, their psyches became the breeding ground of guilt over forgotten acts. Because of all that had happened it had become obvious to them that somehow, deep down, God hated them. Their last thread of innocence was then severed. With that the Hawaiians lost the last of their powers except for the few who went into seclusion. Some never mentioned the old ways again. Others became known as the "dark ones."

In the name of this angry god, all that they had ever held sacred was taken from them. Their sinful bodies now covered, briars with razor sharp thorns that had never been in the Garden before were planted everywhere to make them wear shoes. Every time they were caught celebrating their love with one another they were separated and put into labor camps.

The men were forced to build stone walls on a chain gang—meaningless rock walls that stand everywhere to this day in Paradise, camouflaging the sacred rocks of *heiaus*.

Still the Children of the Rainbow would seek the closeness of their mates to make love. Finally they were imprisoned on the outposts of other islands.

Many died trying to swim the treacherous waves to get back to their loved ones. Those who survived were put to work again building the useless walls.

During this time, two out of three Hawaiians began to die of a mysterious plague. Brought by the strangers it swept throughout the islands. Hundreds of thousands on *Kaua'i* and every other island, and a quarter of a million on the Kona Coast of the Big Island, all perished. It continued until 80 percent of the entire population of the Children of the Rainbow was no more.

Their religion and way of life were outlawed, making it a felony for two *kahunas* to meet or even discuss anything in public. This law still remained on the books of the white stranger's *kapu* system laws until the last decade of the 20th century.

The language itself was also changed to skillfully take the power out of the tone and trap it in the throat so that it wouldn't resonate with the full power. The sacred dance was outlawed as lewd in an effort to destroy the records of their powerful wisdom and the physical connection to higher power.

The last of the good *kahunas* went underground, encoding their chants of the dance and the language itself to be rediscovered at a future time.

Their partial ability to see the future and the remnant of their legends promised that this future time would mark the return of a "Golden Age"—the return of Joy and the healing of the Rainbow Connection with God. Some of this legend was captured on tapa cloth (the first Hawaiian paper) in the last century, never translated into English to this day. These legends, passed down by word of mouth for over 800 generations, as well as the legends from around the world of their lost brothers and sisters, all say that that time of prophesy is now.

 # Three

The Secret of the Hawaiian Mystique

Of course this has only been a story to entertain children around campfires. It has nothing to do with real life and how the world got to the mess it sometimes seems to be in. Such fairy tales of Hawaii couldn't have meaning in the hustle and bustle of our complicated and sophisticated world, could they? But why, then, do all thoughts of Paradise come home to Hawaii? Why is Hawaii the place that most people, if given a blank check, would choose to come to? Is it just the beauty of palm trees and beaches? There are other beautiful islands around the world, many much closer and more convenient to where most of us live. What is it that makes Hawaii so special?

After first visiting Hawaii, I couldn't get the islands out of my mind. Other vacation destinations were checked off like collecting stamps, but I found myself coming back time and again to this most remote place on Earth. It wasn't just the beauty of the islands. There are other places I adore also— the pine trees and mountain lakes of the Rockies of Colorado and Wyoming, the endless red bluff panorama of the Sedona high desert in Arizona—to name just two.

I had been haunted by a vision of Hawaii which began while I was in heavy combat in Vietnam. Because I had never been there, at least in this lifetime, I ignored the vision for years. Going to Hawaii never fit into my practical world. I finally justified it in the form of the traditional vacation. The beauty, and something invisible I couldn't identify, stuck in my craw like a lobster dinner scarfed down too quickly by a starving man. Many years and many trips later I began to consider that the clue to owning that beauty and beholding the intangible was something that I hadn't been able to get in touch with inside myself. Being in a psychological mess as a result of Vietnam I didn't need a Ph.D. to fathom that one. I would have left it at that if the islands hadn't continued to plague me so.

All of my life I have been a "searcher" looking for answers to the secrets and mysteries of life. The older I got the more my efforts slanted towards the search for that "big vacation,"—peace of mind. Ever since my combat experiences in Vietnam I had felt disillusioned. The American Dream was no longer. That war had left me in a straight-jacket which led to a failed marriage. Ten years of every therapy known to man put a tire patch on my psyche. One that still leaked. The best that came out of it all was that Mom was now my best friend, but the flag and apple pie, those traditional values to live for, were gone forever. In a last-ditch effort to find meaning for my life, I washed up on the beach one day at *Kona* on the Big Island.

The sunsets were so beautiful it hurt. That bothered me. Then after a while I would sometimes take them for granted. That bothered me more. Occasionally the effort to remain connected with that beauty got out of hand. Returning from the shortest of trips to the mainland would find me kissing the ground or hugging a palm in front of a departing planeload of startled vacationers. Beneath these awkward public displays and a cartoon Hawaiian shirt there still beat a troubled and unfulfilled heart. As I look back on it I must have appeared ridiculous to the Hawaiians. A *haoli* (foreigner) trying to stay on vacation.

The sunsets got more painful. The evening time for reflection only opened the book on a misspent life. Skeletons poured out of the closet. The guilt flowed over broken relationships and failed businesses masking the real guilt of participating in murder for my country. It presented itself in the quiet time that was supposed to be the relaxation for the soul. I had learned to live with the Vietnam legacy but the long road of trying to salvage a little personal happiness had turned out to be just another form of unsatisfying selfishness. I realized that it would never work for a troubled heart to try and steal a little happiness. Underneath it all I was still lonely and, after having made it to paradise, I was still just an outsider.

One evening, after the painful beauty of God's heavenly easel, a sunset, I wandered over to the shopping complex next door for a snack. Failing sunlight reflected across the silver waves. The air was a perfect 72 degrees. Waterfront row housed the Charthouse restaurant and a half dozen struggling little shops. The blue-roofed complex extended out over the bay supported by huge pylons, an enticing sight, sprinkled with fairy lights. The complex had been plagued with financial problems. The restaurant was successful but the floorplan and its insurmountable flights of stairs discouraged the foot traffic which the smaller shops depended on for their livelihood.

Except for the aroma you would have never known it was there. Wedged in a corner out of the way was my destination: a tiny hole in the wall. I had avoided Crazy Ed's Chicken Shack after hearing that he was a veteran also. The honesty of his business name was surrounded by rumor of his occasional flashbacks from the war. After counseling other vets on the mainland years ago in my own recovery I wanted nothing to do with them. The constant melodrama masking deep hurt was too much of a mirror for me.

A sweaty arm that had just wiped its forehead slapped a small paper bundle on the counter, along with my change. I almost slipped away with my sandwich when a friend popped up.

"Hey, Ed," said Ken. "Pila is a veteran too!" I winced, covering the paper bag and looking for the exit.

"Welcome home!!" came the loud retort from behind the counter. I looked up into a boisterous, ear to ear grin. I was taken off guard by the genuine sincerity. I purposely hadn't noticed the curly, blond bear of a guy in the greasy apron and chef's hat. He stood there in his full body smile, hand thrust out, waiting for a reply. There was an awkward silence. I was stunned by the greeting I had waited two decades to hear. An unsure hand surrendered to his vigorous handshake. Crazy Ed had hit the nail on the head. Only another Vietnam vet could ever know. None of us felt like we had ever really come home.

You just had to like the guy. The sandwich wasn't bad either. I walked down the beach, savoring the last bite, silently hoping that he would always be able to joke about the title he had taken. I sensed the old, familiar turmoil of unresolve in our short conversation. Another vet can smell it through the camouflage of pretense. He was a regular guy on the outside, probably as nutty as a fruit cake on the inside, who had also survived the straight-jacket and pieced his life back together from the only war in history where none of us came back a hero. He had since become the official, self-proclaimed ambassador. He had decided that for the rest of his life, he would welcome home every vet he met. No excuses for what came before and a clear excuse in case he fell down again. The name said it all, Crazy Ed. In the brief moments of joking conversation I knew that he was waiting too, hoping someday to be welcomed home.

I slept on the beach that night. The trade winds were my warm, comfy blanket. Thanks to Ed I had found a clue. It explained the last wasted 20 years of my life. For me all the searching now came down to one thing, finding my way home. "Wouldn't it be nice if it were here?" I said aloud to the goddess of the moon. Under my warm blanket dotted with a million stars, I slept in a closer communion with spirit than I had experienced in decades. The torment of nightmares was soothed into dreams of hope once more. A psychic pathway was opened deep within an untapped region of my mind. I had dreams of the Old Ones, the Ancestors, and a memory of a lifetime, here in Paradise.

The next morning found me fully back on the path of the adventurer. I had never paid any attention to my Cherokee blood. Not even a halfbreed, I now felt native after my communion with the lava and the elements.

Now that I thought I knew the real issue, there was wind in the old sails again. For months I felt genuine towards people. The appreciation for life returned and nothing mattered but now. I took the extra time to converse with others on vacation and a richness and camaraderie that moved us all, emanated from every conversation. I felt like a true ambassador of what we call in the islands, "the aloha Spirit."

I became curious, wanting to know more about the real ambassadors, the "Children of the Rainbow." The Hawaiians have that joy and appreciation for living in the blood. There was something pure about them and the simple way they still lived life that always drew me to them.

I began to study their old philosophy, known as the body of knowledge of *huna,* and was amazed at how little anyone knew of it. Most of it has been labeled "forbidden" in the islands and effectively shoved under the rug. Especially enticing were the stories I would occasionally hear of its magical ability to heal all ailments. The truths I did discover were all profoundly simple, even though sometimes elusive. "Simple" became the guideline for my investigation, realizing that whenever I ran across a complicated truth, it had been bastardized from its original, simple and powerful meaning. The more I researched, the more psychic I became. My dreams became vivid with metaphor.

The first Hawaiian truth about life I learned from an elderly man that some of the villagers had rumored was a *kahuna,* the Hawaiian sorcerer/magician. He was the son of the most famous of Hawaiian *kahunas,* Daddy Bray. Then in his late 70s and health failing, David still had a wonderful demeanor and an incredible twinkle in his eye. Traditional church depressed me but his blessings and baptisms were absolute joy to behold. The sound of his gentle Hawaiian chants made the hair prickle on my arms.

One day when we were discussing the secrets and mysteries, he interrupted me with, "Pila, attitude is everything— that's all."

I didn't get it. From then on whenever the discussion got philosophical, he would cut in with the same statement, no matter what the topic, ending the conversation. Confused at first when it became the answer for everything, I began to think that David wasn't too bright after all. Control of a positive attitude would surely be helpful in life, but not the answer to everything. You couldn't walk through a wall with it or even pay a bill, I concluded. Of course, I was still fairly young back then and stupid.

I next learned the Hawaiian practical application of this most important secret to life from an old Danish sailor named Jack. I had opened up a little curio shop on the main street of quaint downtown Kona. Jack walked in one night and struck up a conversation. I liked him immediately and from then on looked forward to his rare visits. In his 70s, Jack was a Gemini who had traveled the world, always coming back to Kona. He had recently shacked up with a wonderful Hawaiian gal 10 years his junior. They were divorced and widowed and the kids were grown, so I figured what the heck? But their relationship was hit and miss, Jack still maintaining his free spirit at all costs. So far, the wisdom that Jack shared was not Hawaiian—for that matter it was not even wisdom. One full-moon evening he ricocheted into the store, three sheets to the wind: "There is no problem so big that you can't run away from it," he bellowed in proclamation with forefinger in the air. With a sloppy about-face, he vanished into the night for several months. I assumed that the relationship was once again on the rocks.

It was the evening of another beautiful full moon that found him barging in the door again, snockered as usual. Carpenter, painter and master of portable skills, Jack had just returned from another vagabond adventure of working his way around the world. This evening turned out to be a threshold. The celebration of his last male vestige of freedom before throwing in the towel and finally succumbing to the commitment of relationship.

"Pila," he barked, staggering and alerting my customers to attention. "They told me a long time ago what was important and I didn't listen. I have been around the world three

times and the Hawaiians knew the secret all along." Despite
the inebriation I was all ears. "There are only three things
that count in life." He fidgeted with figurines on my glass-
top counter, knocking one of them over. I caught it before
it broke. The customer next to him shrugged and turned
away in disgust. Jack jerked to attention, swaggering, finger
in the air once again. "If you have two of them you can
make it through," he slurred, eyes closed. "The first two are
how you play the game and the third one is the blessing,"
he said earnestly, mustering the authority of a statesman
behind a lectern. The oration continued. "Life is short and it
is over in a flash." He reeled, flailing both arms in an ominous gesture. Two customers bolted and winced as if
preparing for a car collision. "You remember that old song,
'turn around and you're two, turn around and you're four?'"

"Yes, Jack," I said condescending, noticing a genuine
earnestness in my voice in wanting to hear him. "What are
the only three things that count in life?"

"Turn around and you're four," he slurred. He threw his
head back as I braced for the a cappella blast. "Turn around
and you're a young man walking out of the door . . . hey,
ha, ha!" He flailed an arm around my shoulder like a fisher-
man who had just landed a mackerel on a boat deck. The
ordinary world of curio shoppers bristled with embarrassment. I didn't care. I was about to hear three of the secrets
of the Universe. With a big drunken grin he pulled my head
over to whisper the secret. Delivered in a bourbon bouquet
of around 100 decibels, he bellowed, "They were right.
They are always right. 'Turn around and your life is . . .' he
sang, then spoke, "over, all gone before you know." His
eyes then riveted to mine. His words were clear, concise
and sober. I was startled. "And all along the way of life there
were only the three things that counted," he continued in
flawless diction. "Something to do. Something to look forward

to, and the third one, that blessing, if it ever happens . . . someone to share it with." With that statement he made another about-face and staggered out of the establishment. His onslaught, like a wave that had crashed the beach and then sucked out to sea, left a thunderclap of silence, a moment where the utter simplicity of what he said sank in. Disheveled customers returned to their uncommitted window shopping.

Jack must have finally heard what he had been trying to tell himself, because to my knowledge he has never had another drink.

At the time I felt a little let down. I thought that the secret to living on this planet should have been more profound and poetic. As for the bearer of truth, I had learned that lesson a long time ago. The real truths from life don't come to you dressed in robes and walking on water. Too much pomp and circumstance only serves to cloud the issue. A truly wise man once told me, "Pila, I wish that all my lessons were croaked from the mouths of frogs so that I wouldn't consider the source at all and finally know my own truth."

For some reason, the encounter burned into my memory. There was still a complacency that came with such truths that I didn't like, but through the years the full magnitude of their meaning has become an important factor in my search for happiness. Somewhere between the competition of the rat race and the complacency of retirement must be the doorway I had been looking for. That "something to do" and "something to look forward to" had to have drive, purpose and more definition, while I was waiting for the "someone to share it all with."

To this day, more than a decade later, Jack and his lovely Hawaiian lady are living in Paradise. Some of it is spent in Hawaii, but wherever they go, it is Paradise and those whom they meet sense it in the two of them. People who love life are Paradise to be around. It is the mystique of joy that they exude in living a fuller life that I could still talk about but couldn't stay in touch with, let alone exude from my innermost being, as I witness in the local Hawaiian people. What was the formula? I couldn't figure out if that magical quality, that "it" was genetic, inherited or connected with the environment. Hawaiians certainly have "it." It has to do with a respect for life that most of us have to learn and few attain, but "it" is much more that just that.

I particularly noticed this quality one day at a gathering in Washington, D.C. There I was—a fool in a flowered shirt and white pants—trying to hang on to my connection to "it," the beauty and joy of life that I call Hawaii, in the dead of winter. Then, along came "Auntie" (the affectionate Hawaiian term for family when a woman is not of your bloodline), all 200 pounds of her and a smile that brought with it the trade winds and the gentle sway of palms in a crimson sunset. Her joyful entrance wouldn't have been more pronounced with a philharmonic accompaniment. There "it" was, that mystique, drawing you to a hug like a magnet. No matter how they come packaged, skinny or 300 pounds, Hawaiians have "it." In the smile and in the eyes, they carry the music of the islands, the music of the soul, and yes, it is sensual too. In an earthy way, they are very sexy people. How could an entire race of people still, overall, exude such joy after all that they have been through? Sure, they live in Paradise and that is a factor. You must be where you want to be to ever be happy. But the most beautiful stage setting in the world had only dazzled my senses.

The next real clue in my search for the secret to the mystique came when I began to study their language. Again, all the secrets were simple and right in front of my face all the time. The door began to open with two basic words that the entire world knows. Or does it?

The Meaning of Aloha:

I wonder what our world would be like if the words we used to describe it had only to do with its beauty and higher truth? The Hawaiian language is an abstract one of pure essence, possibly the most abstract language known. In the islands the Hawaiian chant is known as the original song to God. You cannot speak Hawaiian without sounding the poetry and beauty of the higher vibrations of whatever you are attempting to describe. Imagine, for a moment, instead of uttering bits and pieces of meaning, having to sing a poetic song whenever you are trying to communicate. The essence of that notion, those pure sounds are captured by the words that make up the Hawaiian language.

Aloha itself has fifty distinct connotations depending upon the context in which it is used. At first this seems vague to the Western mind and the English language which has a concise label for every little thing. But it is not vague when you consider that describing something in Hawaiian will reveal its higher simpler innerconnection with all truth. In fact, blood Hawaiians from the isolated island of Ni'ihau consider English quite inaccurate, complicated and utterly confusing. Our language has disintegrated into an idiomatic mislabeling of things that do not mean what they say. We say things are cool when it has nothing to do with temperature. Now it has come to a meaning of opposites. I began to agree when I saw a Kentucky Fried Chicken campaign featuring their product as being the "baddest" in town. What are we doing to our unconscious minds with this kind of programming? In that vein look at the roots of the English language itself as spoken in Great Britain. It is "awfully" nice to see you and things taste "terribly" good. I suppose that joy can now be described as something "horribly wonderful." And we have the schizophrenia of dual meanings for words. Take for instance, the word "love." To say "I love you" comes with too many connotations to have any pure meaning left. If it is so clear and easy to understand, then why is it so hard to say? Perhaps it is because of the other sexual context of "making love," that sometimes makes it hard for a man to say it aloud. And what about saying it aloud to another man? At times that is almost impossible and may easily be misunderstood unless quite a bit of explaining goes on. How about some of our other sexual words. The one that more graphically describes "making love" is considered obscene and when used in its most powerful form to communicate a negative point, it is actually quite the opposite of love and is considered the greatest of put-downs and a curse.

Hawaiians say that we have chopped up the "song of God" into so many pieces that it no longer rings true in describing anything. We misspell things so that they do not sound like they look with silent letters and consonants that shouldn't be there. From the Hawaiian viewpoint, most of our words have become so digitized, bastardized, chopped up and off-base that they do not sound or vibrate any of the original meaning at all. Combinations of our dribble when used in rhyme and poetry paint back some of the picture but very little. The romance languages still carry a bit of a clue by not killing things in life by referring to them as inanimate objects. In Hawaiian everything is considered alive.

To begin to understand the deeper meaning of the word aloha it is important to know that it does not mean "goodbye." There are no goodbyes in Hawaiian. The concept of separation and endings does not exist in the roots of the original language. At first one might think that would leave some real gaps or voids when trying to describe things, but not if you understand the Hawaiian philosophy of life. Imagine if you lived in a world where no one died and there were no goodbyes. Wouldn't it be nice to know that you were always connected even when you were not physically in the same place at the same time?

The closest thing to good-bye in Hawaiian is *ahui ho,* which means "until we meet again" and more. We will meet again, even if it is in a thousand years, and we will recognize each other (by our eyes.)

Aloha sends with it a connection. It acknowledges "that which animates your heart and my heart." We share in common the living, love force of the Universe that rides next to the breath and brings our heartbeat. We dwell within that same living force and in this word-sound I acknowledge *that* as the blessing and the truth about our coming together or our "seeming" separation. And so, it does mean hello, I love you and it goes with us wherever we are without ever having to say goodbye.

The further clue for understanding the foundation of the Hawaiian language is the composite of the words. Even the pieces of the words hold the meaning. *Alo* means "to be with" and *ha,* well there's a word to understand; a word that is the foundation stone and building block of one of the real clues to the mysteries of life. A clue to the Hawaiian wisdom, the higher connection to the Universe and the power that was once the greatest of all sorcery and magic. Most folks think that the interpretation of *ha,* simply means "the breath." It does, and in that simplicity is the clue.

The secret meaning of Hawai'i

When Captain Cook came with his glad tidings, paving the way for missionaries and a disease that wiped out two-thirds of the entire Hawaiian population, he asked the inhabitants where they lived. By the third island, he considered them rather stupid savages who didn't even clearly or specifically know where they were standing. No matter what island he was on, the interpretation was the same: "I live in *Hawai'i.*"

What the overly educated fellow didn't realize was that the natives were sharing a profound spiritual insight with him. An insight that has completely escaped Western culture to this day. The indigenous Hawaiians were actually trying to convey that they didn't live on a gob of dirt, as beautiful as it may appear. They didn't live on a clump of real-estate like Western man, sectioned into pieces and covered with labels, maps and titles to be fought over.

The Hawaiians were saying that their life force dwells within the one Supreme Force of the Universe and rides upon the breath which brings our heartbeat. That breath is called *Ha*. The third dimensional medium for nurturing and conducting that life force is the water that nurtures life, *wai,* epitomized as supreme causation, know as *"I"*. They were saying that they live, dwell and find their being within the true meaning of Paradise, sustained by the supreme force of the water and breath of life, which is everyone's connection to Paradise who would understand this . . . *Ha - wai - i.* "Where do I truly live? Where do I live, dwell and have my being?" They replied, "Within the supreme wellspring of the life-force of creation that is within me, the all that I behold is Paradise."

As I have continued to unlock the profound wisdom of what I call the Crown Insights of Hawaii, through the years I have wondered how my brothers and sisters of the Earth could have ever been called loin-clothed savages. A power and magic beyond anything ever captured by Western man was inherit in their teaching and way of life. I have discovered that the key to the doorway to all the mysteries lay in the very sounds and intent behind the way they described things. I sensed not only that Hawaii was special, Earth's Crown Mystery, but the people, the islands and the mystique surrounding both were all interconnected. There is a greater hidden meaning for why the whole world is drawn to Hawaii.

Then, when I delved into the mystery of the Hawaiian chant and its affect on the physical and spiritual being, a half-breed Cherokee misfit from Oklahoma began to sew together pieces of my vision of Hawaii from the trauma of combat in Vietnam. Little did I know at the time that peeking into the language would reveal clues to some of the greatest mysteries of both science and religion that have baffled Humankind since the beginning of what we know as time.

Tired of conflict and the competition and madness that society had come to be, I finally felt that I was standing at the threshold of a great adventure.

 # Four

War Is No Fun–
Let the Adventure
Begin

Before I begin to share about the Crown Mystery that is Hawaii and her people, I would like to take you on a different kind of journey. Whether you make it physically to Hawaii or not, there are some things that you will want to get in touch with—things that, from a Hawaiian viewpoint, may help you on your path in this time of great change and uncertainty. For the human race is at a threshold at a most critical time in all history. As a result, people are going through a lot of anxiety right now, and Hawaii . . . Paradise, holds a clue for making sense out of it all. Perhaps this little journey will help that anxiety about an uncertain future and help you and your loved ones in other areas of your lives. Perhaps it can even help you get the most out of what you are looking for in life.

To get the most out of this adventure, you may want to pack differently. I want you to take something with you that you may not have remembered to pack for a long time. Dust it off—it's in the closet somewhere. According to the ancestors (the Hawaiian Elders), it is the most powerful tool you will ever own and your visa to opening all the doors that lie ahead. It is your *childlike wonderment and imagination*. During these times of high pressure and confusion, this is not the frivolity of an old generation of thinking, but your master key to another dimension of excitement.

In this world of chaotic change people are clearly dividing into two camps. There are those of us who have become more fear-based and are withdrawing, retreating from life. They are the serious people who call themselves "practical" by never going forward and by hedging all their bets with extra insurance. Their dreams are based only upon security. Their goals become more and more oriented towards relief from the drudgery of life.

Then there are those who have decided to get on with the joy that life can be. At every age they are realizing that we are entering into a new dimension of exploration. Resistance and competition for them are being exchanged for an all-out embrace of life. For these people of all ages, the magic has begun to pour back into their lives. Insurmountable problems dissolve. From health issues to their pocketbooks, things simply begin to work themselves out. What is their secret weapon against a world of chaos and confusion? It all has to do with attitude.

You heard about the study of the two kids put in rooms full of horse manure, didn't you? An hour into the study a psychologist opened the door on the first kid. He was sitting in the middle of the pile, sulking and holding his nose. They opened the second door and the kid was singing joyfully and digging away. When asked why he was so happy, he replied, "With all this horseshit, there has to be a pony in here somewhere!" An old joke for sure but a good statement about attitude. An important factor that goes unnoticed is about children.

The clue for reclaiming the magic and joy in our lives may has already been discovered by us all and then forgotten along the way. The clue is something that we may have taken for granted. It is a spark of something magnificent that we all have had before life became terminal. Then, through the centuries, serious, educated mankind hammered the joy out of it and squeezed it into a long, arduous path called enlightenment.

The Hawaiian Children of the Rainbow knew all of its answers and more. They knew secrets beyond meditation that led to total transformation. And they knew it didn't take any effort at all. They knew that when you were excited and aware of a few simple rules of the game of life, the door to the answers you were looking for would swing open. It all had to do with that elusive, evasive, intangible thing called attitude. The great masters and sages throughout time have always known that this is the master clue.

"Attitude is everything."

—The Great Sage, Bugs Bunny

"When did the magic go? When did life loose its luster? Oh, to claim back the immortality that is innocence and youth."

When I was a kid in Stillwater, Oklahoma, there was only one big all-encompassing problem for me—boredom. I thought that where I lived was quite ordinary. If you weren't interested in watching the grass grow, about the only thing there was to do was buzz the malt stand. I was too young for cars and girls, so fishing was about the only word of the day.

One day a kid my age from Arkansas moved in next door. Jimmy had red hair and freckles, but that's not what made him special. He was full of energy and excitement, had a keen sense of adventure and above all, a unique way of seeing the world around him. All of a sudden, through Jimmy's sharp vision, my ordinary backyard became an explorer's wonderland.

Until Jimmy came along, when I turned over a rock it was just a rock. All I saw was Earth and an occasional worm. With his elated attitude and keen observation, each rock became a doorway, an "open sesame" to a new world of adventure. Suddenly there were miniature dinosaurs in my newly discovered world (lizards and horny toads to the ordinary eye). Overlooked rock chips were revealed to be ancient relics of real Indian arrowheads. Under my old house we discovered more treasures I had never noticed before—pottery jugs and earthen marbles, fired in the ancient kilns of yesteryear. The pottery marbles did indeed turn out to be a treasure from the more recent days of covered wagons and had lain there unnoticed to the casual observer for over 100 years.

With Jimmy's spark, the imagination of two children painted wondrous pictures of what had come before. Our pirate memories seemed so real that it was as if we had actually been there in a life before, even though we were hundreds of miles from the nearest ocean.

When we became young men, Jimmy and I got a little too serious with life, wanting to do the right thing. I guess we knew something was going on that was out of our hands. We didn't know how big that something was. We didn't know we had picked the only war in history where no one would come back a hero. I made it back from Vietnam; Jimmy didn't. We both learned war was no longer fun.

Today as I think of Jimmy, I know that he would have belonged in this changing world with all its fantastic new discoveries. He would have been in league with Lucas and Spielberg and other joy-bringers of magic to inspire our hearts. Jimmy's spirit was always bigger than any of the little problems of life. He gave me my first glimpse into the importance of the quality of life, rather than playing the game for longevity. I think the Hawaiians were the first ones to say that attitude is everything. I think Jimmy would have made a good Hawaiian.

The world needs an attitude shift right now and could use some of the magic that Jimmy could always see in God's creation. I would like you to remember that notion as you come with me on a unique journey of the mind. Leave the serious world behind for a while. It will be there when you get back, if you want it back.

The Seven Islands of Paradise: Mystical Parallels to the Seven Islands Within.

In my own personal "souljourn" and call home to Hawaii, I have shared many mystical experiences with students and friends. Hawaii is the birthplace and home office for the mystical. In the new dimension of tourism now identifying itself people are coming from around the world to experience this. Since the late 1980s my seminars in the hotels and cruise lines of Hawaii have shown a dramatically accelerated interest in the mystical connection to the islands. This has gone from 10 percent of tourism to an estimated 70 percent who are now noticing something intangible that they wish to get in touch with. To date more than 140 of those whom

I have met also share the same vision of Hawaii that I had in my near-death experience in the combat jungles of Vietnam. It is a very exciting vision of the future having to do with alternative medicine centers and a new thought university to be built here on the Big Island of Hawaii. Many who share the vision have since moved to Hawaii. Could it be that we are all tuning into some sort of a greater unfolding? There are other interesting coincidences that many of the returnees of this strange gathering in Hawaii share. An astonishing revelation for many of us was in finding that our personal sojourns had crossed paths at another time. Before returning to the Big Island, most of the 140 found ourselves on the same trail on the Napali coast on the island of *Kaua'i*. Later I was able to document, through a friend and Hawaiian *huna* researcher, Dr. Serge King, that this trail was used for *kahuna* initiation and enlightenment.

It was on this trail high on the *Napali* coast that several revelations came to me. The first was that Hawaii is more than the most beautiful island chain in the world; it is a living, symbolic metaphor bridging the physical world with the esoteric realm. From that premise came the journey of the mind that has thrilled audiences across the country. I call it the "Islands Within You".

Whether you ever make it to Hawaii in person or whether you have been before and didn't know where (or how) to look, there are some things that you will want to know from the Hawaiian viewpoint. It will make more sense if you begin to see things through Ancient Eyes.

As you travel your own special path in that search to satisfy the heart, there are a few more notions that I want you to consider. They can give you a deeper connection to what we all may be looking for and to the true meaning of the word "Paradise." Let's start with a different look at you. A new look that is actually quite old.

We know now, through quantum physics, that your body is not what it appears to be. It is an energy field that constantly renews itself and exchanges its atoms with the environment. We are now able to measure that exchange rate with radioactive isotopes. Perhaps this is what the Hawaiians have meant for centuries when they say the exhale of each breath is a gift of your magnificence to the environment which then gives you back the gentle blessing of its life-force. An old Hawaiian saying says that when you see yourself for the first time for the *alohi* "sparkler" that you are, you will never have a problem with self-esteem again. When we do not see this way it is simply because of *nana kuli,* lazy eyes.

Science has also finally accepted the fact that the mind is not confined to the brain but extends into the trunk of your body and perhaps beyond. In other words thinking is not produced or even limited to the brain. The Hawaiian priests called *kahunas* knew these things and more, centuries ago, as evidenced in the new interpretation of ancient chants which we will go into later.

There are several "frequencies of knowing" within this energy field that you call your body. For thousands of years Eastern enlightened philosophy has called these frequencies *chakras.* Colors have always been associated with these seven major *chakras.* Now science knows that color itself is a frequency of vibration.

To begin to understand these seven frequencies within you, they can simply be compared to various frequencies on a radio dial. The lower chakras, associated with red or orange, could be equated to AM rock music and the dense, physical, heavy beat vibration, while the higher ones, such as purple or blue, could be likened to FM stereo and perhaps, if you will allow, the vibrations of refined, classical music. One is not better than the other, just different, and has a different function.

One of the basic Hawaiian beliefs is that smaller living things have a likeness to larger examples of life—that is, *microcosm* has similarity to *macrocosm*. The Hawaiians believe that so it is throughout the Universe. Thus came the inspiration of seeing the entire Hawaiian island chain as a living body and comparing it to one's own body or energy field.

If you are willing to consider such a far-out notion, then we shall see if we can discover something new. An old Hawaiian proverb says that great things will happen for us when we begin to understand (or remember) that all of life is interconnected.

And so it came to me, high on that *Napali* cliff, that the living beauty of Hawaii physically represents the living beauty within us that we can all map out and get in touch with—a beauty of spirit that clearly runs throughout God's Creation. I was told psychically that there would be evidence of this connection, little clues throughout the islands on this journey of rediscovery to prove this. Most importantly, it came to me that the islands are an "initiation," a personal "sojourn" for all individuals who wish to become enlightened. I believe this to be the destiny of the Hawaiian islands, for the world to come, get away from it all, rejuvenate the body, mind and open up to spirit. It is the place to process the confusion about the games we lose ourselves in and remember our higher connection. Of course Hawaii is naturally the planet's most remote and perfect sanctuary for this new kind of reflection and relaxation.

The first clue giving evidence of this ancient connection has to do with the colors associated with certain chakras. Throughout history the Hawaiians who love life and understand their relationship to Paradise have always called themselves the "Children of the Rainbow." In Hawaiian legend and folklore, the rainbow was the visible proof in Paradise of the bridge between the worlds of Heaven and Earth. The reason that rainbows were considered the most real of all physical manifestations at one time was because they were the living display of the easel of the Supreme Artist, God. From this arch of perfect order and beauty God is said to have painted all of creation. And of course, Hawaii produces a copious quantity of the most brilliant, hand-painted rainbows in the world.

I then discovered that the ceremonial Royal Courts and *Hula Halaus* (schools of hula) of each islands have colors corresponding to the colors associated with the *chakras.*

The original wisdom of Hawaii, always being simple, knew only three energy centers in the body, instead of the more complicated seven known to Eastern philosophy. A trinity of some sort could be found as the building block in all of nature according to Hawaiian wisdom. (For Hawaiian historians, this simpler understanding of the chakras will also explain the overlap in colors of the Royal Courts of certain islands aligning with the *na'au* (power/heart center.)

Although slightly complicated, the seven chakra alignment can allow a deep, cellular memory activation that you may find surprising by simply dwelling upon the notions that lie ahead. The chants speak of a "spiral within" that holds all the information of all memory, and how to access this information through the breath.

This different kind of journey through the islands (of your mind) has had astounding emotional responses from my audiences who have experienced it live with music or on tape for sleep therapy. I have felt like the Pied Piper taking kids through the mountain to the other side with my journeys of the mind. This stirring of the soul has brought thousands of letters which I will always treasure.

Here, I will walk you through so that you can begin to make your own greater connection.

The Island Chakra Journey

Just relax where you are for a moment. Stop and take a breath and release the tension from the neck and shoulders that comes from reading and intellectual stimulation. My sister once said of a letter I wrote to her, "It made me think so much my hair hurt." Most of the daily tension we experience that is not emotional unresolve can be found in the body from the shoulders up. In a world that is becoming more cerebral this is the tension that feeds a billion-dollar-a-year aspirin industry. This tension can be immediately released anytime, throughout your day, by relaxing for a moment in this manner and taking a couple of deep breaths. We will learn all about the breath as a major key to a greater secret later.

Now, dust off that powerful tool of imagination and pack your bags. Close your eyes for a moment and consider the notion of expanding your body to become large and light enough to float, gently . . . up into the air.

Imagine leaving all your cares and concerns behind you for a while and taking a few moments off to come with me. What the heck, leave the baggage too. Now find the jet-stream that will whisk you all the way out into the middle of the world's largest ocean. With each breath envision your body larger and lighter until your thoughts are big enough to cover the entire Hawaiian island chain. Notice how easy it is to think of your body as large enough to cover the whole island chain because from this high in the air, the islands look like dots in the ocean.

Now descend like a giant silk scarf floating in the breeze, until you can make out the shape of the islands . . . coming closer until you think you see color . . . pastel green in a deep blue ocean . . . getting closer, you can see the mountains now, light green becoming deep emerald green, and your body becoming larger with each breath as you draw closer. Notice the tropical jungle, crystal streams and water-falls, palm trees surrounded everywhere by sandy beaches circled in turquoise waters, encompassed by the vast deep blue, endless ocean. You can now see the submerged coral reefs and the ocean bottom from the air, engulfed in the bottomless deep blue. Begin to feel the warm trade winds. You can almost smell the balmy air filled with the fragrance of exotic fruits and flowers. Float down even closer now and begin to meld, blend with the islands . . . your body large and light enough to encompass them all. In the thoughts of your mind, rest now on your back as you merge with the islands, remembering that this is Paradise and nothing can harm you here. Nothing poisonous, not even snakes exist in Paradise, only beauty, vibrant with life. Look out into the Universe as you float there gently in the middle of the ocean.

The forbidden isle of *Ni'ihau,* is at your crown (top of your head.) The Island of Fire, *the Big Island,* melding with the base of your spine and loins, with all the other islands perfectly aligned in between.

Picture then, a crystal at your crown containing the hidden rainbow of colors that is found in all prisms, crystals and raindrops. Take a deep breath and consider that this island represents all the knowledge that has been forbidden for all these centuries of our evolution until now. Just as the pure-blood Hawaiians are locked away on this forbidden isolated little island to this day, Hawaii itself has been isolated from the rest of the world until the last century.

As you float here in the middle of the ocean where East meets West, gazing out into the Universe feeling larger than life, you may begin to contemplate the magnitude of this tidal wave of change upon us all. You may consider the notion that this may be the most defining moment in all history and a very special time to have been born. Allow the suggestion to cross your mind that finally, after all these centuries, the secrets and mysteries of everything that has baffled Humankind are finally being revealed. Consider the fact that within one spiral of your DNA is more knowledge than all of the libraries in the world and that somewhere within you is a memory and the ability to begin to sort the secrets out and find their greater meaning.

Now consider the purple band of that rainbow that lies hidden within the crystal of your crown chakra—a brilliant, iridescent, deep purple. Imagine that purple band arcing downwards from the top of your head to between and just above your eyes. Now entertain the notion that the unknowable is making its purple connection to activate your third eye which corresponds to our beautiful garden island of *Kaua'i*. It is here, on this island only, that the purple crystal, amethyst, is found. It is associated with meditation and the third eye, the place between and above your eyebrows. Amethyst produces a frequency wave conducive to tranquillity and higher thought.

As you concentrate on the place between your eyebrows and the soothing purple color, know that this is the island where the initiates came to become *kahunas*. *Kahunas* were the powerful sorcerers and magicians of Ancient Hawaii. *Kaua'i* is the "monastery island" for retreat and meditation. It was and is the place to reverse thinking, to see differently, to stand upon the high mountain, to put life into perspective and to reflect upon one's destiny. Legend says that after such a solitary experience, the initiates then knew which island would be their destiny.

Now imagine the deep blue color of the ocean and float your thoughts down to your throat, which is our island of *Oahu,* the voice of the islands where 80 percent of the population resides. The voice of this island is changing. As the voice shifts from male dominance back to female softness the island is experiencing a transformation. *Oahu's* voice is changing back to the original voice of the islands—Her voice. What, then, is your true voice? What are you all about that needs to be articulated? Savor this thought as you would a freshly caught dinner at one of the gourmet eateries in Honolulu. Get the taste of what it is like to speak your own words of wisdom.

Concentrate on sky blue which is the unique blue of individuality associated with freedom. My tribe, the Cherokee, gave turquoise as a gift in this celebration of one's individuality. Later associated with manhood, it was originally given whenever a person blossomed into his or her own sense of who they truly were, no matter what the age or sex. The gift came with this saying:

> "Now you are no longer bound to the Earth or restrained by earthly opinion. Let blue hold your focus from now on, for this is the color of the sky. Lift your wings, for the wind will sustain you like the eagle, and elevate you from the earthly realm. Go, fly, find out now what you are all about . . . and your reason for being here this time."

Allowing your true voice to begin to follow the heart, let's set sail on that deep blue ocean to discover the island of *Moloka'i*. Fill your sails with the pink clouds of an early evening sunset, as you discover the island that is associated with your heart chakra. The only island never conquered by the Polynesian repopulation and the home of the legends of the *Manahuna,* later known as the *Menehune,* or "little people."

Several of those legends say that the islands were once called *Mu* or *LeMuria*. In more recent history, *Moloka'i* became the island of leper colonies, where the hopeless went for their salvation. In spite of the warring, bloodshed and exploitation Hawaii has been through, this is the island that has never been overpowered, enslaved or overdeveloped. She is the heart of Hawai'i—unscarred by the manipulation and will of man.

Moloka'i is represented by the lush green of our life-giving Paradise, the highest physical vibration and the pink of heart-love. The chakra island with two colors. The island where spirit meets flesh, the sign of the cross or the star within you.

With the heart now in charge of the head it is safe to rediscover your true power on the nearby island of *Lana'i*. Beyond the Western misconception, true power lies in balance, living in harmony with nature without turmoil. Home of the Dole plantations, *Lana'i* has been labeled the pineapple island. The bright yellow of pineapples is the color always associated with the power chakra. *Lana'i* literally means "conquest of the sun" giving further understanding of its energy, power and color.

Strawberry papayas and orange crimson sunsets draw us to the sexual chakra and the night life of *Lahina* on *Maui* where the jet-set likes to romp and play. If this flares your nostrils and makes you feel frisky, the key words here are the "appropriate" and "respectful" use of this energy. The understanding of sexual energy may be the most important single factor at this point in our evolution. The ancient wisdom says to feel good about your sexuality. It is the seat of your creativity and the frequency of manifestation.

Another interesting clue to this area lies in the nearby, often overlooked island of *Kaho'olawe*. It is associated with the spleen. Until recently, no one has been able to keep the Navy from using this tiny island for bombing practice. Is this symbolic of man venting his spleen in anger ?

If frustration or anger associated with power has been an

issue, go ahead and "vent your spleen". Take another deep breath and let it all go. Consider the notion that your body knows how to get rid of anything it no longer needs, with each breath, down to the cellular level.

Finally we come to the base of the spine and the fire and flame of the *kundalini* (life force), home of the volcano. This is the island that produces obsidian, the black crystal, heralded in legend as the "mirror of the soul," the *kahuna* stone. In American Indian wisdom, it is also known as Apache Tears, the stone for the healing of karmic wounds. In Egypt and Africa onyx, another black stone, has the same legend associated with it as Hawaii and is referred to as the High Priest or Priestess stone. The black of obsidian and the red of molten lava are the colors that have always been associated with the base of the spine chakra.

This is the island to which I was drawn as a result of my vision in Vietnam. The hundreds of other healers with the same vision call this the island of new beginnings and "the doorway." This is the island of purification and processing. The Big Island may be of critical and timely importance in first identifying the new paradigm for living.

Each island has its special destiny, as does the entire chain. Perhaps they may be the rejuvenation center for a troubled world.

If you find the correlation between the islands and the chakras interesting then you may find that contemplating the chart and finding out a little more about the island that strikes your fancy quite enlightening. Could this be an activation of some kind of DNA or cellular memory? Another of my sojourns of the mind called the "Journey to LeMuria" has had a startling response with 30 percent of all audience experiencing the same memories. This has caused a stir in the professional community and is now the subject of further psychological investigation.

What exactly is this "call home" that is the yearning of the heart for a place called Paradise? What is the strange familiarity that thousands experience when they cry at the sight of the hula or the sound of the Hawaiian chant? Have we come this way before? Were we all once around the same ancient campfire? Hang on—after all, I promised you a different kind of adventure.

Mystical Parallels:
The Seven Chakra Islands of Paradise

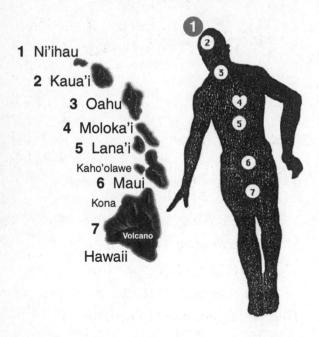

1 Ni'ihau

2 Kaua'i

3 Oahu

4 Moloka'i

5 Lana'i

Kaho'olawe

6 Maui

Kona

7

Volcano

Hawaii

©1990 Pila of Hawaii

PART II

The Island That Has Awakened

*"Welcome to the Island
of Fire and Ice, one of three
doorways on your planet, where
the Earth itself liquefies and
nothing is as it seems.
Here is the gateway to another
dimension and a different reality.
Here, where time itself
has come undone."*

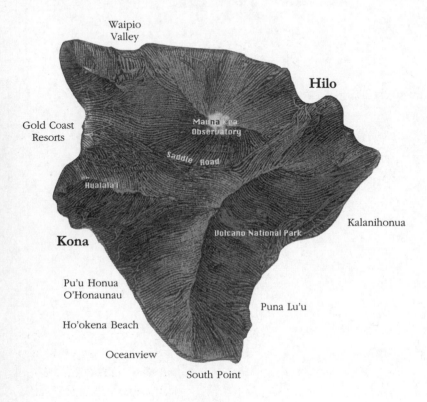

Waipio
Valley

Hilo

Gold Coast
Resorts

Mauna Kea
Observatory

Saddle Road

Hualala'i

Kalanihonua

Volcano National Park

Kona

Pu'u Honua
O'Honaunau

Puna Lu'u

Ho'okena Beach

Oceanview

South Point

The Big Island

 **Five**

The Big Island: Doorway to the Other Side

Now that you have connected metaphorically with Paradise and have allowed certain notions to stir your subconscious, let's take a closer look at the island that I call home. With an active volcano, the Big Island of Hawaii is definitely where the action is. And yet with all the global weather changes and earthquakes, I consider the Big Island to be the only safe place on Earth. The energy seems to be bottled up ready to explode everywhere else. Here, where the energy is naturally vented, is the only safe viewing area for the force of creation.

It is, however, an energy that should not be taken for granted. The key word here, as any resident of the Big

Island can tell you, is *ihi*, "respect." A place of such incredible energy tends to stir deep emotion within the individual and naturally awaken sensory capabilities. It is not a fearful place to live, even though it is the ideal stage setting for the paranormal. As a result this very unique island has become the focus of escalating worldwide attention.

The world's greatest natural phenomenon with its setting of tropical splendor is the perfect breeding ground for myth and legend. You couldn't emulate a better one with a Spielberg budget. That is why the island chain has popularly become the central "on location" movie set of the world. From this spectacular combination of elements, prophecy has been fostered, from the dawn of ancient Hawaiian legend, spilling over into the Western world and the present day.

In the early 1960s Dane Rudyard prophesied that the Big Island would evolve to function in the capacity of a major seat of government (one of three) during the upheavals that would be experienced as the 20th century drew to a close. Interestingly his book, *The Astrology of American Destiny*, has been dusted off and recently released.

Since I have brought up the dreaded "A" word, I had better clarify a few things on the controversial field of astrology.

This ancient feminine (right-brained) science has had a bad rap through the ages. Most people do not realize that astrology has its masculine (left-brained) side, being an exact and mathematical science, probably the oldest. The confusion and lack of credibility has come in its interpretation. Because the gravitational influences of the great clock of the Universe manifest change in every element of creation, opinions on the same astrological configurations can vary from the ridiculous to the sublime. A simple Hawaiian guideline for knowing if you are getting the straight scoop on an astrological aspect is this: If the information is negative, it is not the full picture. There is no negativity in astrology, only energy that is sometimes interpreted as such. Two pitfalls have kept astrology from ever receiving any real public credibility, even though major figures have sought its service throughout time, from kings and queens, to politicians and heads of state. One pitfall is that human consciousness greatly resists the concept of an outside invisible force influencing our lives. Some people feel that astrology can usurp our divine individual choice, which isn't the case at all, if you understand the subject. Secondly, there is the problem of using astrology as a crutch. I know of celebrities who will not go outside and face the day without consulting their astrologer first. To them I say, "Get a life." Astrology is like a map. Like a roadmap, astrology is meant to be a useful tool to help guide you to wherever you want to go.

I do not, however, advocate studying astrology in great detail. I think that, like dissecting the human body or taking apart a computer, it is not necessary to know its minute function to make it work for you. If you knew a few more aspects about yourself and your friends at this deeper level, however, there would be a lot less frustration, conflicts and argument in the field of human relationships. There is a lot we can learn from astrology, particularly in areas where there is no explanation or larger picture. The reason for the quick lesson is that astrology is one of the few explanations for Hawaii's special energy and the role she may play in the bigger picture. One that is becoming the focus of greater attention.

Another great sage and astrologer, Thane Walker, also predicted the destiny of the Big Island in his series of lectures given in the 1960s.

"By the turn of the century when the forming guidelines of society have eroded and become effectual, all eyes will turn towards the Pacific. The Big Island of Hawaii will become the stage setting and processing center redefining the template for living. It will evolve into a voice equal to that of government in a new way of thinking."

Thane was a controversial mystic of the 1960s proclaimed to be "the Teacher of Teachers" by Earnest Holmes, one of the great thinkers of our time. Dr. Walker was a psychoanalyst who took his tenure under Freud and was a personal student of the greatest controversial mind of our century, Gurdjieff of France. It was at a very sobering cocktail party/seance hosted by Dr. Walker in 1965 that I first heard of the prophecy of Hawaii's destiny as a crossroads for humanity during a time of greatest change. Dr. Walker said that Hawaii would be a "lighthouse to a world adrift in unpredictable seas."

Later, in a near-death experience in Vietnam, I had a detailed vision that I believe to be connected with this prophecy. In a future setting of strange buildings and strange happenings, I saw the Big Island as an aperture, the Earth's giant doorway to the Universe and another dimension of reality. After losing my men in combat and getting out of a straightjacket, it has taken two decades of searching to begin making sense of that vision. It still sounds a little like an acid trip, but please bear with me for a while, even if visions and all this psychic hullabaloo are not your cup of tea. More than 140 returnees to the Big Island through the years have had the same identical vision. These people are from all over the world from different walks of life and had never met before. Their backgrounds are as diverse as you can imagine, from architects to doctors to economists. The only common thread I have found amongst us is some sort of near-death experience or radical saturation point or threshold that had happened in our lives. Oh yes, and we have all had a close encounter or two. (You can play the *Twilight Zone* theme music now.) There is something "big time" going on at this precise moment in our evolution and I am firmly convinced of one thing. At the bottom of what seems like two separate worlds of thinking, that of biblical prophecy and the UFO phenomenon, is some sort of Hawaiian connection that may begin to make sense of it all. Wild, huh? I know what you may be thinking: ancient aliens in grass skirts and why did I blow bucks on this crazy book when I could have gone to McDonald's and had a Big Mac? Hang on: I did promise you a different kind of adventure.

The connection may not only have to do with this very special chunk of remote real estate called Hawaii but also with the lineage, legends and belief system of her people. Keep your sense of humor and don't forget to bring that most powerful of tools with you, your imagination. If you can't take me seriously, that's all right. This journey will still work for you if you take it tongue in cheek . . . just don't bite your tongue off if your thoughts hit a bump or two.

There is another way that we can begin to weave the impossible together into a larger tapestry that could start to make sense. It is through a different understanding of the legends and myths we tell our children. What if we took them literally and presupposed that they were based upon fact? Hawaiians say that the truth to all reality lies in the dreamtime of our imagination. They contend that nothing is made up, but "tuned into." In other words, when we create or fabricate, we are actually tuning into the greater reality. This viewpoint is shared with other tribal peoples, such as the Aboriginals of Australia. They call the greater reality from whence comes all, the "Dreamtime."

One simple Hawaiian guideline for getting on the band-wagon is this: That which is precious to our hearts is closer to the truth. That which delights, excites and brings joy holds the thread to the truth and a greater reality. Hawaiians say that thread was once a rope of pure bliss and reassurance, our God-Link™ to the Creator and the Garden of Eden within. Today it is still remembered as the *aka* cord, the shadowy connection, the embryo of essence.

Thanks to Steven Spielberg, John Boorman, George Lucas and other great sages, our art forms have already begun to reestablish these ancient connections and teach a new generation the old wisdom of our cherished legends. Due to the contributions of such joy-bringers we are realizing that so-called folklore, the stuff of children, is riddled with profound knowledge. Obewan Kanobe and Yoda teach us specifics of the Universal Force that is the interconnected energy that runs through all life. Peter is finally exposed as the "Pan" while our beloved Tinkerbell (angel or fairy?) in the movie *Hook* explains her relationship to us and where she can be and always has been located. Pursuing folklore from the point of view of research may hold as many answers for our troubled belief systems as do our precious scriptures. Why? Because that which brings joy to the heart holds the truth.

Bring on more popcorn and do your homework with new eyes, all you old and wrinkled kids. In all this seriousness there may be hope for our world yet. Is there more to "Open Sesame" than just the amusement of an Arabic children's tale? Hawaiian legend says that a tone can alter the body and open the "doorway" to greater realities. Hawaiian chants explain a different look at the origin of life, claiming we are not what we appear to be, but greater than we have ever thought we were. One chant says that we are made up of a special energy force of light that, through a simple understanding, can connect to the place where greater energy dwells.

Power Vortexes

As practical and down-to-earth as society would like to be, there are certain places on our planet where the universal laws of nature that we have come to depend upon simply do not apply. These are known by sages and seers as "Master Vortexes." These special places are said to be the "crossroads" of certain energies. In reference to the human experience, some of these locales are considered unstable, such as the Bermuda Triangle off the southeast coast of Florida and its flip side, the Devil's Sea off the coast of Japan. These are areas affiliated with the mysterious disappearances of many ships and aircraft throughout history, continuing to this day. "Power Vortex" is the popular term for any place of this nature where unusual energy dwells. For the everyday world, these can be considered to be places where "magic" can happen.

A power vortex is where certain energy concentrates itself or comes together. A way to visualize this invisible force is to imagine a tornado or whirlpool. As the energy gathers, it has a central focal point, an eye, which is the stillpoint or void. Becoming psychically aware of where this focus of energy exists is not as difficult as it may seem and we will go into the Hawaiian way of doing this later. It is easy to denote and may be a tool of awareness that you will want to develop to aid you in the future.

Many of the folks that I have met through the years on the Big Island are versed in the subject of power vortexes and what is known as "lay lines." Lay lines are a mathematical grid connecting Master Vortexes and their substations which compose a myriad of junior power centers throughout the world. Lay lines are a way of determining the major crossroads of these energies as well as a way of observing and verifying other phenomena. There has been a major resurgence in this ancient esoteric study which has recently spilled over into our modern scientific community, causing quite a stir. The most startling revelation of this "global grid" was in finding that the ancient sacred sites around the world all sit on precise conjunctions of these lines. In other words the grid reveals some sort of perfect mathematical interconnectedness to the natural as well as man-made sacred monuments of civilizations throughout the ages; civilizations that have supposedly never known each other. (You may now play the *Twilight Zone* theme music.)

Many people versed in the understanding of lay lines and power vortexes have been a part of the unusual gathering on the Big Island of Hawaii. Most of those whom I have met in the last 10 years came heavily credentialed and spoke in a technical tongue barely distinguishable as English. The only thing I have in common with any of them was the brush-with-death syndrome. It seems that we have all glimpsed another reality, are living to tell about it and have this incredible drive to make sense of it all. As I look back it reminds me of the movie *Close Encounters of the Third Kind*. You know, that scene where Richard Dreyfess had been abducted and didn't know it and was compelled to build mash potato mountains in his living room. (I particularly related to the part where his family was convinced that he was "crackers").

One of the egghead faction of our gathering who was into lay lines was a physicist who had worked with the United Nations. Alexandra mentioned in idle conversation that she was also struck by lightning. From the tone of our conversation it seemed like a common occurrence for her. "Oh yeah, I got my Ph.D. from M.I.T., then I got married, then I was hit by lightning." To which I replied, "You must be family. I died twice in combat and Dr. Barry here died on the operating table."

These were not the days of ordinary conversations or meeting places.

This particular meeting was on a fantastically beautiful ranch at the Northern end of the Big Island near the affluent town of Waimea. The town came into being as a result of the Parker Ranch, the largest privately held ranch in the world. The elevation is above 3,000 feet and it is always cool and misty. The vastness of the countryside (not normally associated with the word island) is reminiscent of the green rolling hills of Oregon or Washington state.

I had heard the term lay lines used for the first time at that cocktail party of Dr. Walker's in the 1960s. Alexandra and her associates told us of the planetary grid showing the precise interconnectedness of sacred spots such as the Pyramids of Egypt, Macchu Piccu, Uluru in Australia, Easter Island, etc. to name a few, as well as a connection to the volcano of Hawaii. At the time this was an omen for me since I had intuited the connection from my vision in Vietnam but didn't know why. (Years of mash potato mountains in the living room.) The particular ranch we were on was the 360-acre estate of Woody Woods, an heir to the Ralston Purina fortune. Having the necessary resources, Woody had spent years in selecting this as the best location in the world for everything to do with a sanctuary for living. Alexandra said that the power point on the property was a place that actually defied the law of gravity. I never experienced my body leaving the ground there but the conversation sure did. Still, the greater meaning of lay lines and planetary connections eluded me for many years.

Through those years I had shared the speaker's platform with other scientists and educators who had all brought pieces of this larger puzzle of power vortexes home to Hawaii. One of those enlightened beings is a Hawaiian, a professor at the University of Hawaii, whom I call Ruby. She has come to certain similar conclusions about a planetary grid having to do with sacred sites. Through left-brained scientific logic that has awakened the soul-memory of her Hawaiian blood line, Ruby is reflecting a new light upon the true wisdom of her people. Her theory contends that the

Ancient Hawaiians were psychically attuned to these mathematical alignments called lay lines, and possibly to the
global grid that they compose. She has documented the
incredible accuracy with which *heiaus* (sacred places) align
with the *heiaus* on other islands, an alignment that can only
be verified by aircraft! She has further noted certain interesting celestial alignments, the ramifications of which are yet
to even be fathomed. This is the tip of the iceberg of a deeper
look at the wisdom of a people which Western civilization
still views as somewhat primitive. Ha!

Hawaiian legend and now a new wave of psychic channeling contend that certain of these key vortexes, like the
Big Island, actually stabilize the planet and hold it together
through their grid energy.

Now there is scientific proof unfolding that the Big Island
is directly connected to a place in India (specifically, the
place where 30,000 recently died in the world's most disastrous earthquake) as well as to the pyramids in Egypt.

These three energy vortexes are the master links to other
transformational energy spots that I refer to as the junior
vortexes. The so-called "New Age" movement has given
popularity to many of these places, i.e, Sedona in Arizona,
Taos-Santa Fe area in New Mexico, Boulder-Estes Park,
Colorado, Nelson-Calgary (more precisely the Banff
National Park ski area in S.W. Alberta), Canada, Mt. Shasta
in California, Mt. Ranier in Washington and Tri-pod rock in
New Jersey, just to name a few. The prophecies and my
shared vision portend that these places will act as transit
facilities and half-way houses for our major metropolises
during a time of great transition.

An active volcano pinpoints the Big Island as the major
"doorway" for the hemisphere, consistently held ajar by the
grace of Madam Pele, the volcano goddess of Hawaiian myth.

Other specific identifiable energy centers coexist within

the master vortex, such as the one Alexandra was drawn to in Waimea. Tourists notice such places all over the islands as a pile of rocks that some pagan heaped up next to the road to worship for no apparent reason. Hawaiians know them as *heiaus,* sacred spots.

South Point: The Crack In Time

When I first gave seminars at the major hotels on the Big Island the conservative establishment was split over two controversial issues in my subject matter. The largest resort in the world, the Hyatt Regency Waikoloa, now the Hilton, loved my talks for tourism but pulled me aside when it came to UFOs. "The public will consider it just too weird if you tell them about what goes on here," said the director of entertainment. "We think it would be best to skip the subject."

Then I was interviewed in Kona by a new retirement community for the rich. I was to give a series of talks in the condo sales clubhouse. Concerned about their affluent image, they wanted to know the exact subject matter of my lectures. The gentleman who interviewed me was a well-known retired golf pro, fashionably dressed in leisure wear, flashing a Rolex on a well-manicured hand. After I finished talking I could see that he was concerned. "I don't think it is a good idea to get into all that crap about Hawaiian voodoo," he exclaimed as he ran his fingers through his silver, coiffured mane. "But did you see the UFO that came across the golf course last week?!" I tried to set him up on a date with the entertainment director of the Hyatt but it never jelled. As a result I remained controversial with both camps and decided to write a book instead of giving seminars.

Controversy has always crept into my life, usually uninvited. After Vietnam, I became Chief of Military Police in charge of stationing Marine guards at top secret facilities throughout the globe. Some of the men who later returned to Camp

Pendelton told incredible stories. When these stories first surfaced we hadn't yet set foot on the moon so there was absolutely no basis in our reality to support the Marine's claims of alien encounters and government coverups. Most of their stories were passed off as fantasy and dismissed in ridicule. Along with those rumors came a top secret document. Naval Intelligence had completed a three-year study on the power vortex known as the Bermuda Triangle, the place where ships and aircraft have disappeared without a trace. The inch-thick document culminated in a statement I would have never attributed as coming from the government. The conclusion was that this area off the coast of Florida appeared to be "some sort of rip in the fabric of time."

Thanks to the silver screen and dazzling special effects we are becoming more receptive to the impossible. The creativity of movie makers and other artists has helped the minds of a whole generation become more flexible. This expansion of our sensory awareness may be helping to prepare us for the larger truth of the unexplained phenomena that have persisted throughout our history. I believe that the lid is coming off and by the end of the 1990s the full meaning of UFOs and other mysteries of our world shall come into true perspective, revealing the whole puzzle.

The phenomena which I call "doorways," exists in several places on our planet. Some of these apertures in the space-time continuum "open" in accordance with celestial alignments. They may have been used regularly by "higher intelligences" (for lack of a better word) to travel back and forth.

In decoding ancient Hawaiian chants from a new perspective, I have found what I believe to be evidence that the Hawaiian *kahunas* were aware of this at one time or another.

In my seminars I have shared the ancient Hawaiian wisdom

of huna with 18 other indigenous tribes around the world to date, including the chiefs and medicine men (and women) of the Aboriginal, Maori, the American and Canadian Indian Tribes and the more isolated small island cultures from Tahiti and Fiji to Barbados. It was unanimous with us all that the roots of their teachings are the same. In fun I pronounced them all as being of Hawaiian ancestry, soothing the battlescarred heart of my half-breed, Cherokee self. What was startling was that many of these medicine men and sorcerers were also aware of the notion of "doorways" and power vortexes. Not only that, there was evidence in their stories of an ability at one time to astral travel to and from these special places. From the American Indian Peyote ceremonies to Aboriginal rites, there was wisdom of how to alter the consciousness so that the body itself could pass through certain apertures of the space-time continuum.

I believe South Point on the Big Island to be one such aperture or "doorway." The density of our three-dimensional reality seems to be very thin there and the "glue" that holds that reality together may soften in places like this. The Big Island as a whole has this characteristic of softening the glue of reality, which is not surprising when you realize you are in a place where a volcano liquefies the very Earth itself. South Point seems to be the actual rip in the fabric. When you travel the solitary 12-mile road to this southernmost tip of the United States, you will definitely feel an unusual energy.

Reports of UFOs and strange goings-on abound in this area. Many of the residents down there act weird and they will be the first to admit it. Half of them walk around barefoot in an effort to just try and stay grounded.

One of my favorite stories about South Point is about a woman who was very excited about her move to the Big Island with its UFO sightings and other mysteries. After purchasing a new home, she was enjoying her first sunset on the *lanai* (porch or deck) when a UFO as big as an office building shot up out of the ocean, producing a column of water several stories high. Without hesitation or word of explanation she walked back inside, packed and left the island.

Talking about another reality and actually witnessing it can be shockingly different issues. Sometimes these places will upset the *na'au* (the place of knowing; tummy) to the point of nausea. If you don't mind having your world turned permanently upside down, there is a practically new house with an ocean view for sale near South Point.

I spent the night of celestial celebration in 1987 known as the Harmonic Convergence at this southernmost tip of the United States. It would have been less eventful if I had just downed a dose of LSD instead. The energy is so strange on the South Point plateau, and the winds are so intense that the trees grow sideways. This unusual perspective makes you walk funny when you first get out of your rental car.

South Point is a high cliff peninsula that looks like a huge landing strip. It is reminiscent of the plains of Nagassar in Peru, that special place of gigantic hieroglyphs that can only be discerned by aircraft. Nagassar is another lay line-connected vortex.

As far as I can intuit, this shard of eerie, other-worldly energy runs from South Point through the fresh lava bed settlement known as Oceanview and zig zags up to and through another strange area known as Saddle Road, which is the mountain highway that bisects the Big Island. Although Saddle Road is paved and in much better shape than, let's say, the road to Hana, Maui, rental cars are not allowed up there. They are, however, allowed on the road to Hana. Why? More on this later.

The Big Island has a reputation for being spooky—which is fully justified. Spooky can become exciting when you see the bigger picture.

There is a certain comfort in being within the confines of a modern resort on the Big Island even though all tourists can still feel the special energy. A rental Jeep will easily leave the 20th century behind you for awhile.

Oceanview: The Catacombs And "Now Time"

Above the southern tip of the island is a small village called Oceanview. Built upon a gigantic, jet-black lava flow, it looks like the first settlement on Venus. Accordingly, the residents of this retirement community are all staunch individualists and pioneers who have truly left it all behind. What started as a get-rich scheme for a Florida swamp salesman became the dream for a few special people who have truly got away from it all. The filling station and general store are the last stop for planet Earth. My good friends, the owners of the Texaco station, run a delightful second honeymoon bed and breakfast. Drinking champagne in their hot tub, there in the middle of nowhere, underneath the clearest sky you have ever seen, will convince you that you have gone to another planet. There are at least twice as many stars in the sky there and because of the location the crescent moon and celestial configuration are all upside down!

Oceanview is as undeveloped as real estate comes. In this story of creation, God had a touch of Alzheimers. In the third day, he forgot to come back to the sand box. It has an unusual beauty, though, and was probably where the word "rugged" was coined. The elevation is a couple of thousand feet with miles of crisscrossed, semi-developed roads stretching from the mountain horizon to the ocean. Talk of a Riviera Hotel has remained just that, the funding mysteriously interrupted through the years. I think the residents would like this last frontier to stay unmarred by the candy wrappers of humanity. They have hidden a most beautiful green sands beach there, barricaded from the public and a secret to the hotel developers and most of their own population. Because of the lava flows, traditional sandy beaches are a rarity on the Big Island but they are special and come in three colors. This little oasis is emerald with olivine. Sometimes called peridot and known as "the Luck of Pele," this is one of the few natural crystals of the so-called youngest island. The lava of the entire community is permeated with these tiny green crystals of volcanic glass.

Beneath this rather eccentric community is another unusual secret, often overlooked by the populace. Here lie thousands of miles of great cave-like tunnels known as lava tubes. There is much legend surrounding these labyrinths, which were formed by the cooling lava. They are said to riddle the islands and even interconnect them. They are also the resting places for the pre-Christian Hawaiian dead. Unlike other caves and tunnels these caves have no echo because of their porous lava rock composition. To enter them is an eerie experience.

The expert in the field who mapped many of the lava tubes is a retired Coast Guard officer named Dwayne. He can usually be located through one of the local cafes and will sometimes conduct private excursions. Dwayne and his son have personally plotted thousands of miles of these tubes that riddle the islands. Whenever a new tube system is discovered on the construction sites of new buildings, his team is called in to map them and ensure that Hawaiian grave sites are respected and left undisturbed.

It is known that the first hospices for the gravely ill were founded in caves. Because of the negative ions in the air of the lava tubes, bacteria will not form in a laboratory petri dish. The Hawaiians call these negative ions the "breath of Pele." Post-operative complications due to infection, which

plague Big Island hospitals, would probably be nil if surg-
eries were performed within these caves. Could it be that
the Ancient Hawaiians knew this?

Another interesting overlooked characteristic of the lava
tubes are their occasional columns. After you have explored
miles of tubes emptying into cathedrals the size of the
Houston Astrodome, you will encounter this absolute, pol-
ished smooth, tapered column. In the midst of a jagged,
porous pathway they look man-made, as if a modern artist
had sculpted giant spindles and placed them as support
columns. And support they could. They are solid steel,
unmelted by the 3,000 degree lava flow that created the
tubes. The iron ore content is so dense that this southernmost outpost of the United States is known to throw off the
compasses of passing ships and aircraft. The Space Shuttle
uses this point to reorientate their instruments whenever
they lose contact with Earth.

I would suggest that if it were possible, all vacations or
study retreats to Hawaii start and end with an excursion into
the lava tubes. The experience quickly strips away 20th century awareness and all that complicates and preoccupies the
mind. Similar to a *samadi* (flotation tank) experience, the
deafening quiet of the "now moment" is indeed an intense
meditative experience, particularly for those who have trouble
focusing their attention. I call it the thunder of one hand
clapping. Whether you are at the end of your life or at a
new beginning (called *huina* in Hawaiian, both are considered the same threshold or *puka*), the lava tube encounter
makes for quite a threshold experience. It can be a tunnel
towards the light.

Hawaiians have a name for experiencing the pitch black,
soundless lava tube. It is called the "Now Time Experience."
It is also interesting that the Hawaiian language itself contains no past or future tense, only present—only now. An

old Hawaiian proverb states that we can never return to Paradise until we stop dwelling in a past that is dead, a future that is only a dream and begin living in the eternal now. The chants say this will bridge the two into reality and bring back the gateway to immortality.

The Crystal Connection

"Gifts of the Earth, flowers that do not fade. Clues to God's perfection, grabbers of light, communicators he has made."

Speaking of lava and crystals, allow me to jam another whole seminar into a few paragraphs about crystals. After all these centuries they are now in vogue. You can experience a deeper, intuitive connection while in the islands, or wherever you are for that matter, by a simple understanding of these marvelous, natural tools.

Crystals are easier to work with than most of the hocus-pocus you may have been heard about. They are a direct *nature-link* to the invisible, higher realms and can rapidly help you develop your psychic abilities. Developing your sensitivity to extend beyond the normal five senses is necessary to participate in the new dimension of exploration now upon us. Indeed, as we continue over the threshold of our physical world into a mental one, psychic ability may even become necessary to our very survival. Everyone is equipped from the factory to do this, proven by the fact that we are only using an estimated three to five percent of our natural capabilities. You don't have to be weird like me or have a near-death experience to awaken these qualities.

If you are new at this and want to give it a shot, go to one of the several crystal stores in the islands or find one of the 2,300 coast to coast near your home. Start with any plain, raw (unpolished) quartz crystal shard that you may be drawn to.

There is a saying about crystals: You will be drawn to the

one that wants to be your friend. Crystals are never lost but they do find new friends when the time comes. In other words, one that you need to work with will be hard to lose and you will not be able to hold on to one that needs to go to someone else.

To trigger right-brained intuitive thought, simply hold the crystal in your non-dominant hand and study its tip. This works great when you are in a non-thought specific, day-dreaming mode. Vacations and lounging around a pool or on the beach are perfect times for this.

Crystals have a natural balancing and soothing effect which explains some of their appeal. Humans know instinctively to go to the beach to soothe and balance themselves. Just like a puppy knows to eat grass when he is sick, humans instinctually know that the beach will make them feel better. The sandy beach is pure crystal silica even though less vibrant than larger pieces of quartz crystal. The black sand beaches of lava here on the Big Island are special in a different regard. We will discuss that quality later.

The precise angle that natural quartz terminates in can be a key to unlock the mind. For those inclined to Jungian psychology, the natural quartz termination is like an archetype symbol to the unconscious.

This specific angle, which is accurate within three decimal places, is also what causes quartz to aggravate its surface electrons providing it with its special energy known as piezoelectricity.

To charge your crystal with the wisdom of a place, simply leave it there overnight, preferably on black lava. Then work with it in the above suggested manner or leave it under your pillow for a few nights.

To avoid nightmares, pay attention to your *na'au* (gut feeling) toward the place that you have visited. *heiaus* (sacred sites) are full of this information. Be thoughtful as to what may have gone on there. *Caution: Do not disturb or take things from these places.*

The closest thing in nature to quartz is the gray matter of the brain. When a crystal heats up in your hand or gives you chicken-skin you are communicating with it, accessing its stored information or feeling its reaction to the environment.

Sulfur, Oklahoma: A Crystal Connection

The "New Age" fascination with quartz crystal is not something this movement discovered and is certainly not new. It is not as complex as some might make you believe. Crystals have been around and helping people for a long time. I knew about them when I was a child.

I was born in Sulfur, Oklahoma, a sister vortex to the Big Island. Sulfur is a little-known place and known only to an obscure work called *Emerald Tablets* and the brothers and sisters of the Hawaiians, the American Indians. American Indians of all tribes would come to the area now known as Platt National Park, located at Sulfur, to gather crystals. They would come to this area of the Oklahoma "bad lands" no matter what warring was going on.

Here they would set all weapons aside and relax in the healing waters together. Legend has it that they would sit in the hot springs and talk of the place where we all came from—a garden without winter, located in the middle of the ocean; a place of rich unlimited bounty without poisonous vipers or dangerous beasts.

The Arbuckle Mountains near the park's hot springs are solid quartz crystal and amethyst. My grandfather, a full blooded Cherokee whom I have come to know in spirit, taught me about crystals and their use. I have found that Hawaiians use them in a similar way. In spirit, he still works with me today in the old native tradition of communing with the ancestors. I use a technique known by my tribe and the

READER/CUSTOMER CARE SURVEY

HEFG

We care about your opinions! Please take a moment to fill out our online Reader Survey at **http://survey.hcibooks.com**.
As a **"THANK YOU"** you will receive a **VALUABLE INSTANT COUPON** towards future book purchases
as well as a **SPECIAL GIFT** available only online! Or, you may mail this card back to us.

First Name _____ MI. _____ Last Name _____

Address _____ City _____

State _____ Zip _____ Email _____

1. Gender
- ❏ Female
- ❏ Male

2. Age
- ❏ 8 or younger
- ❏ 9-12
- ❏ 13-16
- ❏ 17-20
- ❏ 21-30
- ❏ 31+

3. Did you receive this book as a gift?
- ❏ Yes
- ❏ No

4. Annual Household Income
- ❏ under $25,000
- ❏ $25,000 - $34,999
- ❏ $35,000 - $49,999
- ❏ $50,000 - $74,999
- ❏ over $75,000

5. What are the ages of the children living in your house?
- ❏ 0 - 14
- ❏ 15+

6. Marital Status
- ❏ Single
- ❏ Married
- ❏ Divorced
- ❏ Widowed

7. How did you find out about the book?
(please choose one)
- ❏ Recommendation
- ❏ Store Display
- ❏ Online
- ❏ Catalog/Mailing
- ❏ Interview/Review

8. Where do you usually buy books?
(please choose one)
- ❏ Bookstore
- ❏ Online
- ❏ Book Club/Mail Order
- ❏ Price Club (Sam's Club, Costco's, etc.)
- ❏ Retail Store (Target, Wal-Mart, etc.)

9. What subject do you enjoy reading about the most?
(please choose one)
- ❏ Parenting/Family
- ❏ Relationships
- ❏ Recovery/Addictions
- ❏ Health/Nutrition
- ❏ Christianity
- ❏ Spirituality/Inspiration
- ❏ Business Self-help
- ❏ Women's Issues
- ❏ Sports

10. What attracts you most to a book?
(please choose one)
- ❏ Title
- ❏ Cover Design
- ❏ Author
- ❏ Content

TAPE IN MIDDLE; DO NOT STAPLE

BUSINESS REPLY MAIL
FIRST-CLASS MAIL PERMIT NO 45 DEERFIELD BEACH, FL

POSTAGE WILL BE PAID BY ADDRESSEE

Health Communications, Inc.
3201 SW 15th Street
Deerfield Beach FL 33442-9875

FOLD HERE

Comments

Hawaiians as *Moe'uhane,* the "waking dreamtime." Through the wisdom of our ancestral bloodline, I have come to know the simple knowledge of crystals. Crystals are our communication link with the Earth Mother.

My work with crystals has brought me to the realization that the human race has come beyond the Nuclear Age and is in the first phases of the Crystal Age.

Legend has it that we have come full circle to the same knowledge and threshold of the original science that blew up Atlantis. The first actual manifestations of this new age were not just long hair, weird clothes and hippies talking about good "vibes"—but computer and satellite technology as well. Everything that we are experiencing in the new dimension of communication and virtual reality is because of the simple quartz crystal.

The piezoelectricity in quartz is the simple ability to attract, store and transmit light by resonance. Resonance is the fundamental conductor and building block of the Universe. Science still cannot classify light as to whether it is a particle or a wave. The answer is yes. It is both. The building blocks and nature of the Universe are described clearly in the ancient Hawaiian chant.

The Pyramids of Hawaii:

One of my first psychic intuitions about the Big Island came with several prophecies that happened before I permanently moved there in the early 1980s. In a daydream while humming a Hawaiian song I saw three pyramids in a triangle grid around the Big Island. The understanding that came with it was that the pyramids were holding the volcanic energy safely open in some sort of a doorway between dimensions.

It came to me that one of these pyramidal structures was in the beautiful Valley of the Kings, on the Hamakua Coast,

Waipio Valley, and that it was a gateway to the underworld. Later I discovered a rather distorted Hawaiian legend that also tells of a doorway to the underworld located in this valley. This ghost story says that if you wander into the cave at the base of the pyramid, *menehunes,* the little people, will grab you and pull you down into the underworld. These stories abound throughout the islands in regard to certain labryinths, such as the wet caves in *Kaua'i* where many people have disappeared throughout the years. Another local legend of the Big Island calls the guardians of the Waipio Valley cave the "mole people." Still another campfire story of old from that area depicts the guardians as aliens from another world who have been living there for millennia.

I have never actually seen this particular pyramid of my dreams but keep hearing rumors of its existence from the residents of this mysterious and most beautiful of all valleys. There is a large lake at the far end of the valley and I sense something special in the jungle whenever I hike near there. Soon after the first hiking trip across the valley an old *kahuna* told us that this was where the pyramid is located. Whether it evades this dimension or is actually an earthen mound to the ordinary eye I do not know. It doesn't seem that the jungle could hide it even though the area is dense in undergrowth.

Lifting the Veil of Reality

The second pyramid was found exactly where I had intuited its location to be some 10 years prior. Along the southern coast of the Big Island past South Point there is another energy spot of incredible beauty. Whenever I travel as a passenger or drive by this place, it will pull me out of a trance, out of a sound sleep or out of a conversation and turn my head nearly off my shoulders. It has done so ever since my first trip to the islands. I knew there was something beyond the force of its incredible beauty to draw me there. It is directly above the property called Punalu'u where I have dreamt of founding a resort/conference/healing center and "new thought" community for the arts.

In the misty clouds of the mountains I have "seen" the tiki torches of a beautiful restaurant and retreat along an airstrip. This is part of the vision that has haunted me since before the Tet offensive in Vietnam, half a lifetime ago.

The pyramid itself was most recently discovered by an Apache sister who has stewardship of some incredible sacred ground a few miles south of there in a place called Wood Valley. Her stewardship is at the top of a triangle of loamy soil that is thought to be part of the original *LeMuria* never covered over by the more recent lava flows that have caused the island to be labeled as young. The pyramid was found after hiking through miles of logging roads hidden by giant stalks of sugar cane.

When I discovered the pyramid for myself, I was standing with friends in a sugar cane field, high on a logging road in the mountains, talking with cane workers. I had hiked there many times before to no avail. The mountains are always heavy laden with rain clouds giving the scene a surreal quality with limited visibility. This day the clouds parted suddenly and there it was, looking exactly like a replica of the Great Pyramid of Giza. The feeling was a rush like Ronald Coleman must have felt in discovering the passage opening up to Shangri-La. I still get gooseflesh when I think of it. The cane worker said, "Oh, I never noticed that before." He yawned and scratched his head. We almost wet our pants.

The pyramid is quite large, symmetrical and flat on top. Natural formation structures like this are known in the islands as cinder cones, where lava swelled to the point of almost exploding and then subsided, sometimes leaving the structures hollow. Two things made this one unusual, besides being the subject matter of my visions for years. Other cinder cones are all round mounds. This one stuck out like a geometrical building. For me the second interesting thing came after trekking up to the base of it. The pyramid is hollow and you can hear a waterfall inside it.

It seemed at the time that you could reach out and touch it but it was actually miles away. I came back later with hiking gear and a picnic lunch to explore the new find. The cane fields were horrendous enough but the last mile was pure impassable jungle. After losing my direction and then my way altogether, I finally ended up in a clearing at the base of the pyramid just before sunset. An ordinary hike had turned into a sojourn, like trying to conquer Everest. I was bruised and scratched and very worried about making it back without becoming lost again. Behind me now was the 20th century and before me a spectacular natural wonder that seemed from another time and place.

Hawaiians plant a large leaf shrub called *ti* as protection around their homes to ward off evil spirits. The ti leaf is used in all rituals of purification. The plant itself is usually up to six feet tall, a single white stem with a bundle of large leaves at the top, like a round bouquet. Here before me, like giant ominous tiki torches guarding a palace, was a perfectly aligned stand of ti plants at least 50 feet in height. This jumbo floral arrangement made the whole scene appear like a surreal oversized movie set. It felt like King Kong would appear at any moment. The ti leaves stood like the flags of the United Nations—guidons before an unearthly monument. I felt like an ant in the land of giants.

I paced the clearing in front of the pyramid wondering whether to go on to try and climb it. Because it was late I decided against it, but something else happened. For some reason I was moved to chant Hawaiian, a dedication, something to commemorate the event. The sound was deadened, my voice with the magnitude of an ant was lost in the air, until I reached the center of the base of the pyramid. Then, all of a sudden my chanting rang out with an echo that, later I found, could be heard throughout the valley. Startled by the rebounding resonance, I turned and squinted into the failing sunset. Far away, down the mountain to the ocean was the tiny village of *Punalu'u*. I was in direct alignment with the village and the place on the highway that had always turned my head for all those years since I first came home.

I believe the waterfall inside the pyramid mountain is a wellspring that feeds the beautiful forest leading down the mountain range to *Punalu'u*. The forest is quite old with large emerald green pines, ironwood and redwood trees. Robin Hood would have felt at home here. From this perspective it looked as though the pyramid was the fountainhead of the entire forest and village miles below, giving life to both. *Punalu'u* means to immerse oneself in the wellspring of life. The resort has an unlimited spring water supply that bubbles up on one of the few black sand beaches left in Hawaii that has not been covered over by recent lava flows.

From time to time ever since the discovery, I have been able to see the pyramid through the clouds from the beautiful golf course by the ocean in the *Punalu'u* village. The area is riddled with gravesites and a major *heiau* lies in the forest near the lagoon. If you are attuned to spirits and respectful you will not be afraid. For others the pure "aliveness" of the area is unsettling, as are many of the areas on the Big Island. This area was the inspiration for a recent best-selling novel, a Stephen-King-type thriller on Hawaii called, *The Fires of Eden* by Dan Simmons.

Through the years I have decided that the village with its breathtaking view into the mountains is my favorite spot in all the islands. My brothers from the island of Barbados agree. Resort development in the area has failed. It was recently resold but I have a feeling that nothing major will go on there without respect to and permission from "the other realm." Bobby, a University Professor from Barbados, made a statement in one of our seminars when he first came to Hawaii. He said of his homeland, "I am from Heaven, and I am here visiting Paradise." The audience laughed but Bobby was serious. He later said when visiting *Punalu'u* and witnessing its beauty, "If you had blindfolded me and dropped me here I would have thought that I was home." Of all the indigenous peoples proud of their own homeland who have visited Hawaii, this was the highest complement paid by another.

On a clear day when those rain clouds high in the mountains momentarily lift, it is one of the pure blessings of living in Paradise. For brief moments when I see the pyramid that had eluded me for so long, it's as if the gods are up there in the mountains saying "peek-a-boo" from another place and time.

Perhaps there is nothing ordinary when we truly learn to see with different eyes. Perhaps the wonderment has been there all along. I am reminded of the first sailors who discovered the crater of Diamond Head on *Oahu*. To their dismay its slope of diamonds, glistening in the sunlight, turned out to be quartz crystals. How could they have realized that their eyes were witnessing a psychic vision of the future? They were seeing for the first time what was to become the most expensive piece of real estate in the entire world and the diamonds of a New Age.

What else was there to behold of the monument that stirred my soul which was an ordinary hill to others? I have had other experiences related to the pyramid of *Punalu'u* before I ever actually witnessed it in the three dimensional world. In 1972 I found myself naked by a swimming pool in Palm Springs "toning" Hawaiian. With gooseflesh to the point of almost fainting, I knew that I had stumbled onto a major clue and connection to enlightenment but didn't know why. This was only a small harbinger of visions to come. In 1982 I had a vision of a *kahuna* "toning" the "open sesame" before this very pyramid that I would not actually see until many years later.

Through the reverberation of sound I saw the *kahuna* exciting himself and his body-energy field. Through the years I found clues in science and myth. This was the way of rearranging his molecular structure whereby he was then able to walk in an oblique angle into the pyramid.

Since moving to the Big Island I have heard the legend from three different sources on two islands. It says that when a *kahuna* would take the strange breath and make the tone (and then the tone would make him) he could enter into another dimension and go within the angled hollow mountain. It is said that once inside, untold riches would be revealed beyond the imagining.

This remarkable valley was once home to over 812 ancient Hawaiian families. You will feel the energy of the departed ancestors throughout this area. If you ever have the glorious freeing experience to drive around the Big Island, stop for a while in this beautiful place of sugar cane fields and macadamia nut orchards. On your way to the volcano, rest at the side of the road. Witness the vast, awesome beauty and "tune in" and meditate. You will realize that you have come a long, long way in the journey of life to a focal point of reflection.

Tourists are allowed to visit the nearby Buddhist Temple at Wood Valley. The beauty of this quiet sanctuary is the essence of the serenity found in this valley. No matter what your religion, please be respectful. The monks there are in constant meditation and believe they are helping to hold the planet together. You will fall in love with the forest setting and its beautiful albino peacocks.

As for the third pyramid of Hawaii? It is on the Hilo side of the Island near one of the most beautiful waterfalls in the world . . . if it exists. For it also has eluded the ordinary world . . . so far.

Six

The Connection
with the
Great Pyramids

One of the most interesting people I have met who was drawn to Hawaii was an Egyptian born and raised in Cairo. Fadel was a former Egyptologist who had worked with the Smithsonian. One night, before he was to give a lecture I was sponsoring in Kona, I introduced him to Hawaii's Living Golden Treasure, Uncle George Na'ope. From the moment they shook hands it was as if the whole room shifted. At the old Kona Lagoon Hotel in a bar scene of 100 people you could have heard a pin drop. We knew this was to be no ordinary meeting. There was an unusual camaraderie with the Egyptian and my favorite Hawaiian and we all talked into the night. Fadel confirmed my first clue of Madame Pele's connection with Giza by stating that the literal interpretation of pyramid and volcano are one and the same. Both are feminine symbols having to do with the vortexing of energy from within. I told them of an intuition I had that the volcano of Hawaii and the Great Pyramids of Egypt were the balancing king-pin, Yin-Yang energies for our planet. They both agreed that there was something to this. It would be years before a startling scientific evidence would surface to confirm this beyond our wildest imaginings.

As a member of the Egyptian Department of Antiquities, Fadel had already startled the conservative scientific community with his theory that the seven temples of the Nile were used as Chakra Initiation Centers. In a fascinating slide presentation the next evening, he revealed more shocking realizations. It was a most perfect evening under the Kona stars that the little community will never forget. He disclosed the findings of a French team of scientists who had discovered a new antechamber in the Great Pyramid. They had accomplished this by drilling holes into "dummy" walls that had defied x-ray. This discovery revealed a substance verified as "not of this planet." From another pyramid on the west bank of Luxor came the pictures of extraterrestrial Egyptian gods. Hieroglyphs of giant androgens adorned the walls, substantiated also by the Egyptian Book of the Dead, which spoke of stars as not being objects in the sky but "doorways."

Uncle George, Fadel and I somehow knew that the Egyptian Pyramids and the Big Island had a celestial relation of some kind that was interconnected with our "junior" vortexes, such as Sedona, in Arizona, Tri-pod rock in New Jersey and so on. We knew that it would all come to the light someday and perhaps even reveal our real origin, which we believe is not of this planet. Of course it could all just be the bar talk of guys who were a little strange to begin with. Uncle George and I never felt like we belonged on this mudball in the first place. At that time back in the 1980s

I don't think we ever really knew just how strange it would all become before making complete sense.

The Connection to Eternity

The verification and deeper understanding of the Big Island as being a major chess piece in the earthly scenario and a "doorway" to another, surfaced years later in a scientific body of work so elaborate, precise and profound that it challenges the most creative concepts of science fiction. The first wave of avant-garde thinkers had been wandering around the planet looking for enlightenment on mountaintops from Peru to *Maui,* as well as the artificial mountains of Egypt and Mexico. The Jose Argilles event of the century, the Harmonic Convergence, had flopped for lack of physical phenomenon. Meanwhile, consciousness shifted quietly and universally and the world would never be the same again. The few who had drifted over to the volcano had indeed "felt" something, but for some reason the word did not spread. I was convinced by then that the Big Island of Hawaii was the place that the individual must physically connect within a kind of personal initiation as preparation for the turbulent years ahead. I had personally assisted with many miracle healings here by then, and had seen hundreds of others find their direction in life just by coming to the island.

My introduction to the new body of evidence that scientifically proved why the Big Island is so special to the Earth came through a learned friend of mine, Dr. Gilroy, a retired Harvard Professor on the Big Island. Fed up with the rat race Gil had intuitively built his mansion in Paradise to get away from it all. Without ever saying so publicly, the real motivation was to survive what he considered to be the possible collapse of society. His fortress had also become home to a marvelous hobby, a priceless library of esoteric studies. Added to this life-long collection one day was a thick book entitled *The Monuments on Mars,* by Richard C. Hoagland. My interests at that time had shifted away from unearthly phenomenon and into a more practical phase of my life so the topic was of no interest to me initially. Since my vision in Vietnam, I had grown weary of being accused of having my feet firmly planted in the clouds. I had therefore divorced myself from the "space cadet" crowd associated with UFO escapism, with one exception. Because of Gil's learned and social background I had been tempted to lend an ear to the subject now and then. Gil was a thorough researcher and his documentation and cross-referencing of topics made for a raised eyebrow now and again. Gil always took the extra step when he was excited by a work and had tracked down the author of *The Monuments on Mars.* He and Hoagland quickly became phone pals.

An Evening to Remember

One evening Gil summoned me to dinner and a video presentation that he promised would blow my socks off. He refused to tell me the subject matter on the phone. I assumed that it was because of my recent skepticism and prepared myself for a night of conspiracy and UFOs. In the months of seclusion in Paradise I had become a hermit and was reluctant to invest a whole evening away from my writing. But his French love, Annie, was a wonderful cook so I went.

Once on the road I began to enjoy the drive up to the mansion. The subdevelopment of artists and eccentrics where Gil lives is hidden in a rain forest at an altitude of about 1,800 feet. It is always cool and moist there, in contrast to the beach weather, and was particularly so at that time. The previous two days of August heat and humidity had been almost intolerable. Although I had grown accustomed to the few weeks of extreme temperature in the southernmost island, I always preferred the cooler *Mauka* altitudes. *Mauka* can be translated as "the mountainous areas where God would choose to dwell." I hoped that He wouldn't mind the extra company this night.

A rain shower on the way produced a brilliant rainbow, leaving behind thoughts of an unfinished manuscript. "God, it's beautiful," I whispered aloud. I smiled to myself, mocking a deep baritone voice, "Thanks for noticing kid." An invisible weight I hadn't been aware of lifted from my shoulders. That always happened whenever I took the time to just get out and reconnect with the beauty of the islands. I backed off the gas and whistled my way up the glorious jungle highway.

After 20 minutes of driving I turned down the entrance into the subdevelopment. The tropical flora was exceptionally rich in green against the contrast of a new blacktop road. The air was pungent with the aroma of fallen fruit. The fragrance of rotting bounty along the roadsides always plagued me with a cloud of thoughts of the homeless and starving people of the world. I turned down the final winding drive, dispelling the cloud and claiming back my right to the beauty. Giant wrought iron gates of the Gilroy estate changed my helpless humane thoughts to selfish envy. Gil had it made. He was living every man's dream, retired on a fabulous estate in Paradise while still in his 40s. Every inch of his eight acres had been coiffured to produce food crops. His palace was practically self-sustaining, including the nice tax break that came with having a working farm. Seven species of banana trees graced both sides of the entrance road. The retainer wall was bright orange with huge pumpkin squash contrasting the deep purple of mammoth eggplants.

Tommy, the German shepherd, barked his territorial greeting. High on the 60-foot *lanai* stood Gilroy's final word for Paradise. Packaged in a lovely pink sarong, Annie waved, giving her warm smile. Her informal graciousness always made me feel like royalty. Aromas of Annie's culinary skills enriched the cordial conversation. I could tell that Gil was holding back and was excited about the video he wanted to show me. I was honored with my own personal jumbo mug of fresh herbal tea grown from the garden. We sat at the table under a cathedral ceiling as the taste buds of my dull bachelor lifestyle were aroused in quiet ecstacy. I was soon fully into the physical pleasure of savoring the wonderful dinner and forgetting about the rest of the world. The meal, the setting and the company made for an ambiance that was a feast for the gods.

Tonight was about to take that meaning a step beyond.

I sat on the couch with a toothpick like a satiated male chauvinist pig while our hostess did the dishes. Gil popped the cassette into the machine. I balked at the credits as they displayed the same title as the book, *The Monuments on Mars II*. Heck, I thought. Right when I was enjoying the simple pleasures of Earth, we have to go off to woo-woo land. Noticing that I was disgruntled, Gil reassured me that the evening would be well-spent.

Thirty minutes into the film I was a convert and a changed man. As I sat there with my mouth open I wasn't sure what was happening. The presentation was so elaborate and scientific that it crept into my consciousness, shifting my entire foundation of knowing. The video was unfolding as the missing piece for all the answers I had been looking for since my near-death experience in Vietnam. A larger missing piece than I could have ever imagined. As I watched, something was happening to me at the core of my being, a deep-down feeling that was completely unsettling.

The presentation began with the author's recent speech to the United Nations. It was an exposé on a 10-year scientific investigation that began when the Viking space probe sent back a strange photograph, now known as "the Sphinx on Mars." I had seen this controversial picture on the cover of one of the "rag" magazines in the grocery store years ago and had passed it off as nonsense.

Hoagland, a former investigative aid to Walter Cronkite, was also part of the Voyager Project that sent the first voice mail out into the Universe for E.T. to phone home. He had spearheaded this project, putting his reputation and 10 years of his life on the line. At first the strange photo on Mars was thought to be a trick of light and shadow but Hoagland wouldn't let it go at that. He researched the film library of the 80,000 photographs sent back by the Viking probe and found a second picture of the monument. It was clearly a giant, Egyptian looking mask, several miles long at its base, sitting alone in the Martian desert . . . well almost alone. Nearby stood a visibly clear complex of pyramids. Even though the photos were distant, these shapes could be seen as definitely unnatural to their surroundings, as well as artificial to the normal characteristics of topography and weathering.

This was fascinating enough but what really started things rolling was when someone on the Hoagland team noticed a mathematical correlation between the pyramidal complex and the so-called Martian Sphinx. A mapping of the sites revealed precise trajectories and angles throughout the complex. Excitement brewed in the international scientific community when these mathematical correlations were seen to be redundant. That is, the same precise geometry was repeated over and over again throughout the configuration, with astounding precision to seven decimal points of accuracy. The odds against such things accidentally happening in nature were impossible. Because certain things were repeated, it intonated that a code or signal was trying to reveal itself.

Another revelation came when a member of the team toyed with the photo of the sphinx. Half of the photo folded over disclosed a shockingly self-evident feline/hominid connection which is the cat/man combination, a master clue to ancient Egypt itself and the largest of earthly monuments and enigmas, the Sphinx.

Famous scientists from around the world were drawn to Hoagland's project. Other discoveries snowballed into a body of controversial evidence that sat the scientific community on its ear. A renowned rogue scientist from Hoagland's group postulated a theory that the Egyptian Sphinx is at least three times older than has ever been considered. It was then proven, through a new system beyond carbon dating and accepted on worldwide television. Because of this startling realization, a big problem surfaced that had the scientific community fuming. Now there could only be one civilization responsible for the construction of the Sphinx. The only civilization ever mentioned that it could be pinned on was the mythical Atlantis. Could the mythos of Plato have a basis in reality? This dreaded "A" word had the worldwide scientific community smoking from the collar. It is absolute taboo to talk fantasy to scientists.

As a true professor, Gil paused throughout the video and displayed documentation of his own personal research. It drove each point home like a stake through the heart of my old constructs and beliefs.

Next came the quantum leap in the project—the connection bridging the two worlds beyond anything ever imagined. On an inspirational fluke, one of the Hoagland team made a transparent overlay of the mathematical grid of the Martian complex. He began placing it on some of the sacred sites of Earth such as Stonehenge, reducing it to fit, looking for any kind of correlation. At a 14:1 scale, the master key was revealed to be near Stonehenge, the neolithic henge, Avebury, largest of all known stone circles. When shrunk the diagram fit perfectly, denoting certain geographical points with the same infinitesimal accuracy. The site proved to be a perfect analog, a scale model of the complex on Mars, constructed here on Earth in our distant past. Had ancient astronauts left unmistakable clues throughout our solar system? A trail of clues that had waited for all these centuries until we were evolved enough to figure them out? The implications were now earthshaking, infuriating the conservative community of world scientists. Was the history of our world a misunderstanding or a coverup? Is our origin on Earth not what we thought it was? What were the religious implications? The Hoagland team had become the thorn in the paw of the established order, threatening the very basis of reality. Words rarely uttered from the mouths of gentlemen now echoed throughout the learned halls of academe. "Turn off the VCR," I barked at Gil, "My hair is smoking!" I had to talk a while to air things out before continuing the video. "Good Lord," I continued, stunned by the implications of the film. "Do you know what this means?"

"You ain't seen nothing yet!" was Gil's reply.

"Do you remember Kubrick's *2,001: A Space Odyssey?*" I stammered.

"Yeah, the symbolism of that obelisk that he used throughout the film."

"Yes, yes, exactly!" I gestured, both arms flailing, trying to put my finger on something that I couldn't quite nail. "I saw that film after Vietnam and darn near wet my pants. What's the connection here. What the hell is coming down with all this?!"

Gil was right there with me. "I told you it would blow your mind. Hang on, there is more. The obelisk was used throughout Kubrick's film as something that aliens left behind to stimulate intelligence . . . a kind of homing beacon of enlightenment. There was one at the beginning of the film with the scene called 'the dawn of man.' Then, you remember one was discovered when man went to the moon and so on." I nodded, bobbing like a cork. "Just consider this next factor and remember it as we finish the video. The original inspiration for Kubrick's film and the book that it was based upon, and I have documented this, was a pyramid, specifically tetrahedron, not an obelisk. Now watch." He hit the remote. I could barely sit still. (I have distilled parts of the two-hour message into my own interpretation here as Hoagland continued his address at the United Nations.)

"So, what were the mathematics of this complex in a remote desert on Mars trying to tell us?" Hoagland said from the podium. "The redundant angles repeated over and over again all seemed to say, 'Look to your tetrahedron.' Now what the hell could that mean?" He continued as the lights were turned down in the Dag Hammershald Auditorium and a large screen displayed the planet Mars. "We then took an imaginary tetrahedron and placed it within the sphere of Mars, oriented due north in accordance with the axis and rotation and guess what we found. The base of the triangle, the tetrahedron, whenever it is placed in any sphere came out at precisely 19.5 degrees latitude. When this was done with the sphere known as the planet Mars, one point of the base of the tetrahedron came out on the latitude that is the complex and the Sphinx on Mars. The other angle terminates precisely at the largest dormant volcano in our solar system, a huge mound about three times the base of Mt. Everest. There is nothing else on Mars that comes close to the striking topography of this huge mountain.

"That's not all. When this imaginary tetrahedron is placed in every other planet in our solar system some sort of strange similar energy phenomena can be witnessed at precisely 19.5 degrees latitude. On Jupiter it is the famous eye of the storm, a constant swirling mass big enough to suck up the Earth itself. We think that this energy phenomena we are witnessing at precisely 19.5 degrees is an inwelling and outwelling of energy from another dimension. When the tetrahedron is placed within planet Earth, you guessed it, the Pyramids of Egypt and the Great Sphinx can be noted. And another point of the base of the tetrahedron comes out smack dab at the *Kilauea* volcano in Hawaii."

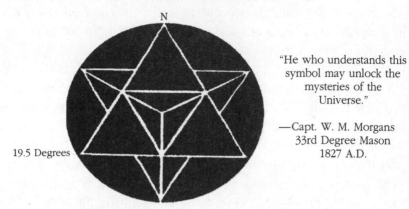

N

19.5 Degrees

"He who understands this symbol may unlock the mysteries of the Universe."

—Capt. W. M. Morgans
33rd Degree Mason
1827 A.D.

I was covered in gooseflesh and the hair stood up on the back of my neck. I looked at Gil, stunned. "Turn it off for a moment!" I said. "This is too much to assimilate all at once, even though it is something I have been waiting to hear for over two decades!"

"No, there's more!" Gil insisted. "This study has begun to unravel everything, from ancient myth to UFOs. Watch!"

By the time I finished watching the video my hair was practically on fire. Other impossible coincidences were revealed, such as the steps of the ancient pyramid of Mexico called the stairway to the gods. The top stair is at precisely 19.5 degrees. There was even a connection with the recent crop circles that have mysteriously appeared in England near Stonehenge. They began the month we returned to Mars and the mathematics were the same tetrahedral geometry, just as if someone were in another dimension drawing them for us to see on a giant Etch-A-Sketch.

I left Gil's house that night numb with questions. I have

since seen the video over a dozen times and I am still learning from it. This profound body of evidence is the focusing lens for a larger picture unfolding on our planet than I could have ever imagined since the vision that altered my lifepath in Vietnam. The full magnitude of Hoagland's work has yet to be fathomed and it is my contention that it shall prove to be a foundation stone of an entirely new approach to our history and perhaps even the origin of the human race.

Soon after seeing the video I began a nationwide lecture circuit culminating in a trip to the eastern seaboard. On that circuit I emphasized to all my students to get a copy of this video for their home libraries. I feel that it must go into the consciousness of as many people as possible. It has been deeply rewarding to be instrumental in presenting *The Monuments on Mars* video to large groups of aerospace workers as well as the staff and employees of corporate industry across the country.

At the end of a year on the road I found myself on my first trip to New York City. It was here I finally met the writer and producer of the book and videos, Richard Hoagland, now head of a team of international scientists who call themselves "The Mars Mission." Since then I have had the honor of being on the same speaker's platform as Hoagland at the New York Whole Life Expo. What was a mild interest in progressive thought, the symposium that year experienced its largest turnout of over a half-million people.

We do not know what the full implications of the Mars connection are as yet but we do know that they further substantiate Hawaii as one of Earth's Crown Mysteries and a doorway between dimensions. Hoagland's website is a landfill of info: www.EnterpriseMission.com. (I like independent viewpoints and always recommend that you ponder as many as possible.) A cool site that boils it all down is: http://dudeman.net/siriusly/cyd/).

Seven

Liquid Earth— *Ho'ihi*

(To Treat with Respect as Sacred or Holy)

Volcano: Sojourn to the Doorway of Creation

So what about this mysterious aperture in the Earth, this doorway to another dimension? In Hawaiian legend, Madame Pele is the symbolic "goddess" of all physical manifestation and the *Pu'ao* (womb) of the third dimensional experience. She is the doorway between realities and Earth Mother of all myth and folklore. Please do not take your visit with her lightly. You are on "new turf" when you visit here and the comfort zone known as your ordinary world no longer applies.

If treating certain phenomena as an entity is awkward or offensive to you, just approach it from the Jungian psychological standpoint of "archetypal energies." Madame Pele is symbolic of the feminine force of all creation, the birthing energy that draws together, vortexes thought into focus and produces physical reality. Archetype means that She is the epitome of such.

Here nothing is dormant, covered up or idle. All that has come before or since is stripped away to where you are getting in touch with absolute raw "source." Although my personal encounters with Pele have involved facing fears beyond those I felt in Vietnam, it is my firm understanding that she is not an angry goddess. However, through facing those issues that are referred to by the misunderstood and degenerated term "fear," you will quickly come to understand its higher meaning.

Ho'ihi

After a close encounter with Pele one geologist said "You could do a lot worse than to worship her as a goddess. She fits all the requirements of deity."

Contrary to early missionary belief, the ancient Hawaiians believed in the One Supreme Being, God-force of all, whose very name was so sacred that it was rarely uttered in public. They also recognized and honored the god-like or archetype energy in all things. Furthermore, they symbolized it artistically in the *tikis* you see everywhere in the islands. Every detail of these carvings represents something symbolic. Even the statues, headdresses and eyes are meaningful representations of certain aspects of the archetype (god-like) qualities that the Hawaiian *kahunas* were focusing upon. They were aware of the invisible laws of nature and were able to symbolically capture their essences in this manner, as we shall learn more about later.

On the Big Island, you are on special ground in an activated time in all history. You are at one of the few doorways in your reality where even the Earth itself liquefies and nothing is as it may seem. That is the reason I feel it is paramount for individuals to come here and experience the energy in person at least one time. Simply having your physical being (which the ancient Hawaiians and now modern science knows as an energy field) near this vortex of raw energy is a form of personal initiation. One that is held sacred in the Ancient Tradition. I cannot begin to tell you in this short book of the number of miracles of healing and manifestation that have taken place here, sometimes simply by realizing the notion of leaving it all behind and stepping out of the old reality and standing next to the pure energy of all creation.

Pele's lava is a powerful symbol and the foundation of new beginnings. Electromagnetic and crystalline in structure, it acts as a "field" for the piezoelectric "armature of you," amplifying what you are all about.

Because of the mysterious force of raw, awakened creation, the island has had a bad rap. To the uninitiated who do not realize what they are dealing with it has been called a place of bad luck and unfortunate happenings. This can now all be explained. For those who truly understand and respect Pele's energy the symbol of a simple piece of lava can mean "on this rock I build my church," or "reality—a foundation stone for a totally new beginning." If this is the case, obey the guidelines and have the lava blessed by a *kahuna* . . . if you can find one to do it. I would rather that you understood the symbolism. Sooner or later, you have to own it inside anyway. Getting the message? If you were able to pick up in your hand and hold the essence of an archetype energy, this is it. It is straight from the other side, not tempered with age or the density of this world.

Here, at the source of creation where the dense, solid elements are liquefied, the doorway between dimensions can exist. Part of the noticeable energy you feel when you first set foot on the Island of Fire and Ice is best described as "the loosening of the glue of your reality."

One of the two important stones produced here is obsidian, the *kahuna* stone. Called Apache Tears by my tribe, it has the same legend wherever it and other black stones are found worldwide. Like onyx in Egypt, the sister vortex of the Big Island, it is called the High Priestess Stone. It is also said to be the "mirror of the soul," held only by the *kahuna* or high priest, the only ones who would dare behold their own dark sides.

There is one Hawaiian craftsman who is brave enough to work with lava. His name is Rocky and he can usually be found in the marketplace in Kona and I highly recommend him. Just as a jeweler facets crystal, the lava has a singular "tamed" *mana* or energy when it is worked. In that sense it is safe for your stewardship as long as you take into consideration all that I tell you. If this sounds like hocus-pocus, bear with me or ask any local resident about the hundreds of stories having to do with lava and the Big Island.

For those who insist on seeing what they can get away with, *BEWARE.* You may be faced with all your suppressed stuff at once and you will learn the word "respect."

During the last active flow one poor soul got his feet burned off. Before that, a European charging for unauthorized private tours to the flow fell through a thin crust in the lava and burned to death while his group looked on helplessly. A personal friend of mine recently pushed his luck a little too far in taking pictures of the flow at sunset. The cliff he was standing on, fell seven hundred feet into the boiling lava. His body was swept out to sea and never found.

I apologize for the graphics, but I still have students and

tourists who refuse to listen. Although considered the safe viewing site for the force of creation, it is not a place for games. I get these little packages with letters of apology back in the mail constantly. I am worn out from taking looted lava back to various locations, particularly after I have educated people otherwise. Understand that this is the newest foundation stone energy on the planet and it cuts through all trite, surface actions or games that have come before. If you think that you are just handling a rock, then you might as well have picked up a chunk of radium. If you have been close to Pele's energy you would know why we call her *Wahine Kapu,* the unknowable woman, mistress of the things of the night, that which cannot be manipulated or controlled.

Recent and profound interpretations of Pele's Chants predicted the direction that the lava would flow over 150 years ago. These chants also foretold the loss of homes in the Puna district, an event that made world news.

Through respect and understanding, the ancient Hawaiians (and some to this day) had a great ability to work with this force. There is a startling recent example of this at the current flow site on the Chain of Craters Road. Where the lava covers the highway you can witness this profound and mysterious human-spirit connection to the energy. The lava flow, several miles in width, came down the mountain devastating everything in its path, including the melting of automobiles and a metal-framed building. Then, when it came to a small house and *heiau,* the entire river of lava split apart, barely scorching a tiny wooden sign at the corner and then came back together on the other side of the *heiau* platform, flowing onward to the sea, and continuing to devastate everything in its path.

I am working on several levels of interpretation of the Hawaiian Chant that specifically deal with how to get in touch with that energy and "flow it." My study is in its adolescent stages and it is with great *ihi* (respect) that I share the following:

Madame Pele: The Ritual of Manifestation

The ritual of manifestation is to be performed only after you have established a personal connection with the island. You will know when that has happened because you are no longer a tourist in the crowd and are filled with awe and a sense of destiny and longing.

The ritual is best performed near one of Her active flows on its way into the ocean or even by helicopter. If you are not able to approach a current flow, you may visit "Her Majesty" at her abode in the *Halemaumau* Crater. This is the crater within the crater, as easily seen from the Volcano House Restaurant. It is visible on all maps and easily reachable by car and a short, fascinating walk.

You may have heard that *Pele* likes gin and cigarettes as an offering. These are indeed fitting gifts, especially if they are symbolic of vices you are giving up. A flower *lei* or a single flower are also respectful. Don't worry about feeling silly—I even had a team of lawyers do this ritual.

Thoughts of all the beautiful gifts that have been given to us by Mother Earth are appropriate at this time to help get you into the proper mood and focus. It is also appropriate to make your gift biodegradable in a conscious effort to do your share. There is an old saying: "That which is necessary to survival has a tendency to become sacred." Ecology is definitely part of the new dimension of our belief system, no matter what your religion and will help you get in touch with the *ihi* (respect) so important to the basic Hawaiian and indigenous attitude towards life.

Your most beautiful outdoor memories will help you fully

focus and "align" with Her energy. Perhaps your favorite memories are of the islands. Or, your thoughts might go to the Rockies, pine trees and clear streams, or even to a farm memory from childhood—whatever brings you the feeling that we call "Aloha for the Earth Mother."

After your offering, go to any of Her nearby steam vents. They are everywhere in the park, a constant, ethereal reminder of the energy of creation. If you witness the flow or see the caldera by helicopter it is best to make note of the moment when you had a close enough encounter to shake the core of your being: The moment that your mouth drops open and you feel uneasy about your safety.

It is said that when her energy is powerful enough to bend the knees and tilt the head back in awe and respect, you are then in the proper attitude to ask for anything that you would have manifested in your life. This excludes nothing. In the Bible it says: "Ye ask and receive not because ye ask amiss." Ask then, from your heart and it shall be given . . . here at the very doorway of creation itself. So be it.

A powerful Hawaiian chant for your prosperity goes as follows:

E Laka E
E Laka I ka Leo
E Laka I ka Loa'a
E Laka I ka Wai Wai
Me ka Mahalo ihi

Hawaiians didn't mess around when it came to asking and manifesting. Their aim was straight to the point and the source. The first line of the chant, *E Laka E,* calls on the archetypal feminine energy of attraction. The essence of this energy is the same as the essence of sexual energy that attracts all mating.

The next line, *E Laka I ka Leo,* has to do with truly striking the tone or hitting the frequency that the name of what
you wish exists upon. A Hawaiian proverb says that you will
never own anything that you can not clearly name. That
defining name has a ring to it that carries its spiritual call.

E Laka I ka Loa'a is to immerse yourself in the river of its
wealth to the point of opulence. To connect with the flow
of the energy of what you are asking for, now that you have
called upon it and defined its current.

E Laka I ka Wai Wai means to allow the river of energy
that is connected to manifest and what you desire to run
through you, instead of just remaining in the dream state.
This is the subtle step forward that eludes most dreamers,
separating them from the doers; those who have tasted and
felt the ecstacy in their minds of what it could be like to
manifest what they desire and those who say that they have
"made it happen." Through this immersion, allowing the
sound of the ancient words to ring with you, you retain that
which is yours out of the sea of wealth you have called into
your being. In other simple words, to connect with the river
(the sound and the intent behind it), you will get wet.

Finally, the last line of the chant, *Me ka mahalo ihi,* gives
respectful thanks for what is to be received. It blesses and
sends the energy back to source, acknowledging the connection and allowing the current to continue to flow.

If there are questions or concerns about ritual I will try to
answer them later. Ritual is a powerful omen to the subconscious mind and the greater part of our being as now
proven in modern psychology. It is important to note that,
from the Hawaiian viewpoint, there is no power in the ritual itself or the setting that you have chosen to evoke it.
These things are all tools to enable you to get in touch with
your own power, the power connected to the higher power,
the life-force essence. This comes through a sharp, singular

focus (provided by the best of stage settings and clearest of fundamental sound and intent) until the greatest of all magic in the Universe occurs . . . your acceptance of your own good. This is based upon universal scientific principles of the Universe that Hawaiians originally knew that anyone could align with. That is all that has ever really happened with anyone who manifested, from Henry Ford to Ted Turner. What they did with it from there and our opinion on whether they deserved or not isn't the issue. The fact is that some time or other this acceptance and alignment happened with those who are great manifesters. The Ancient Hawaiians knew the principles and how to make it easier to focus, that's all. There is an old saying that magic works for anyone who knows the secret.

The Lava Kapu:
A Deeper Understanding

One of the first legends that you will hear about over and over again on the Big Island is that it is bad luck to take lava. I have touched on this before but what many people don't know is that this *kapu* (forbidden rule) and others were lifted just recently by enlightened *kahunas* with certain guidelines.

Please respect where you are when you make it to Paradise, therefore *do not take lava from the Big Island and under no circumstances take lava from a heiau or sacred spot*. Under certain *specific* conditions, I had supported taking lava until recently. If an individual was terminally ill or at an intense "threshold" in his life, I allowed it with a commitment and a responsibility. Because some individuals (who considered themselves "enlightened" and should have known better) took lava without having met the above conditions, I have now decided against it. As I said before, I am tired of receiving the lava and your letters of apology in the mail and then having to truck it back to where it was taken.

At Volcano National Park Visitors' Center there is a drum full of letters of apology with tales of mishaps and woes that accompanied returned pieces of lava taken without "Her" permission. One such person had such bad luck he even sent his tennis shoes with an apology, thinking that there might have been bits of lava still stuck in the soles.

Pu'u Honua O' Honaunau, the Place of Refuge, has a pile of hundreds of pounds of returned lava. It is now called "Gilbert's *heiau,*" named after the park supervisor.

For the person who is living a lie or holding on to anything that is no longer valid in his life, the lava is a living symbol that will bring it to the surface so it can be gotten rid of. As I mentioned, *Pele* is the manifester, the goddess, the Earth Mother. From the depths of the unknowable She has brought into reality everything that you see around you . . . for that matter, everything on Earth.

Those who live here know that it is not an easy place to dwell. If people come here to run away from something, the very thing they are avoiding will present itself for their inspection. The energy of creation is an emotional one. It is our emotions that drive us and this is the home office for letting them rip. People who try to suppress things don't last long on the Big Island. "It" will soon "hit the fan. If you have any "Edge of Night" or "Secret Storm" going on, good luck. You have picked the perfect place to get rid of the soap opera going on in your life. As we say here: Tune in tomorrow for "As the Lava Flows!" if you are ready to let it flow out of your life.

If you feel you were "called here" then there is a simple speedy process for you to get on with your magnificence. You probably already know it—for you were the one who, after planning for the vacation, found yourself dropping all your preconceived plans and peeling away from the crowd.

You found your emotions erupting as if a distant trumpet had sounded, calling you to the lava at sunset. And there you are, barefoot, in tears with everything welling up inside. It may have started when you first stepped off the plane in Kona. Or the feeling may have caught you off-guard when you saw the hula, even though you may have seen it many times before. Perhaps it was a simple Hawaiian song amid the tropical beauty and, all of a sudden, there was a lump in you throat. If so, this is the beginning of your "call home"—not necessarily to the island outside, but to the Paradise within you. To you dear one, *Aloha*.

# Eight

The Crossroads

Honaunau:
The Crossroads of the Universe

If you were able to travel physically to the Edge of Eternity, it would be located 20 miles or so south of the bustling village of Kailua-Kona. Known as the Place of Refuge, *Pu'u Honua O'Honaunau* is also a place of miracles. It is now preserved as a federal park and is easily found on all maps of the island.

Honaunau is the wonderful setting and energy vortex for those who have not been able to get out of their own "soup." Those who have witnessed the raw splendor of this most beautiful setting will never forget it. Even the unenlightened do not take it lightly. It is the only true Hawaiian sanctuary of forgiveness remaining intact on all the islands. The ancient Hawaiians held this place in the very highest regard, as do their descendants to this date. This is the sacred ground where an offender of any act could be forgiven and absolved.

I have been taking terminally ill people to this sacred ground for healing since 1986. The real miracles of the heart come easy in this incredible setting. I promise you, no matter who you are or from what walk of life you come—you will never forget this place. The actual ground of healing energy extends from the beach into the mountains some five miles in the shape of a triangle.

People who have worn out their options have changed their lives forever by making the sojourn to *Pu'u Honua O' Honaunau.*

The actual forgiveness ritual which came to me psychically, received a lengthy blessing from David "Pappa" Bray, the son of one of Hawaii's greatest *kahunas,* Daddy Bray to whom this book is dedicated in memoriam. This special event took place at the baptism and child christening of the daughter of our mutual friends, Mark Victor and Patty Hansen. There were about 35 people present at the event, including a well-known religious leader of our time. Intuitively I described the healing ritual and declared that at least a million people would be coming to the Place of Refuge in the next decade to receive their initiations and healings. David blessed this proclamation with a 15-minute Hawaiian mantra, and then gave me the great honor of allowing me to meditate on those sacred grounds with Daddy's amulet, which was the recipient of Daddy's last breath. I considered this an honor because Hawaiian tradition teaches that the amulet contains the spirit and teachings of Daddy Bray as passed on to his chosen one. Passing the breath from one generation to the next is the traditional way for *kahunas* to transfer their wisdom to the designated heirs of their knowledge. Whether by artifact or from mouth to mouth, this ritual intent has to do with the core-level understanding and fundamental Hawaiian teaching that all wisdom and connection to spirit can be found within our "breath of life." While meditating at sunset on the lava, the amulet heated up in my hand and vibrated. I felt a deep emotion and knew that something special had happened.

That night at the celebratory baptismal dinner, the Hansens asked David about his amulet. David lost his voice and I was able to interpret all the symbols, intuitively. We realized that something truly significant had happened this day as David again gave one of his beautiful Hawaiian blessings for what had happened.

As a result of the events of that evening, I conceived the idea for the first Hawaiian *huna* Intensives to be held at the Keauhou Beach Hotel on the Big Island. I later met the man who would be instrumental in that regard. Tad James was one of the 140 individual initiates who came to me to be taken to *Pu'u Honua O'Honaunau*. He had this to say of the experience: "The top of my head disappeared for six hours!" In a financial crisis at the time, Tad has since built his empire, becoming a major voice in personal, transformational psychology.

Since then thousands of individuals and conference participants have experienced this ritual with wonderful results.

Tuning into the Deeper Connection

The most effective time for the ritual of healing and "housecleaning" is around sunset at *Honaunau*. Arrive at least half an hour before that time. If the park entry cubicle is closed, please leave a donation in the box anyway for this is the only income that the park has. Even though the official hours end at 5:00 P.M. you are allowed to remain on the grounds until midnight. *Please respect where you are and do not disturb anything.* When you enter the grounds you may wish to ignore the recorded button messages, for they have to do with more recent, Polynesian *kapu* understanding of the grounds.

Stop at the entry, take a breath and center yourself. If you are with someone, stop talking and split up. Students of *huna* will know how to take the "special breath" and will want to experience the rest of their sojourn in *hakalau* or expanded awareness.

For the uninitiated this is called the "learning state," which emphasizes a noticing of what is going on in the soft vision or corner of the eye.

There are two distinct "energies" you may notice within the park—that of tall, solemn guard-like entities and that of small scurrying forms, which nature folk-tales would define as *menehunes.* Both are in stewardship of this sacred spot and are to be referred to as "friendly" spirits. Just behave yourself!

There are two other phenomena within the park that some of the rangers even admit to witnessing. One is of a white-robed specter up to 30 feet tall walking on the water or through the grounds. This has been identified as the Christ, a member of the White (Light) Brother(Sister)hood or your own High Self, depending upon your belief system.

Many of my terminally ill clients have said it looks like me and I have been happy to be there for them in any context; however I would suggest that it has more to do with the threshold they are experiencing at the time. Thanks for the thought anyway, but I'm just an ordinary guy trying to get along just like you. So, look again and see the light within yourself.

The other phenomenon has to do with a ball of light that travels throughout the park, on the walls and sometimes out over the ocean. Not much is known about this and its labels are varied, including UFO. Should you see it, let it be a positive sign for you. If you are new to this otherwordly sensation, then take another deep breath and relax whenever you feel uneasy. This is truly a place of love even though it will appear alien and surreal at first. After that first feeling will come a feeling of strange familiarity and longing. Look for it. Feel it. You are about to be welcomed home, to the Edge of Eternity, a place beyond the games and roles that you have had to play in life. A place beyond the walls that man has built to house God. A place where you can begin to hear and heal all that has come before.

Your destination is beyond the hut surrounded with tikis, at the point of the great lava flow that juts out into the water. The remains of some 22 *Ali i* (Royal) Chiefs were once in that hut. Some of their *mana loa* (spiritual essence) is still there.

You will most likely feel something at the hut also. You may want to pause and reflect before going on. That point is like a lightning rod of central focus energy.

Beyond the hut is a *tiki* who is physically excited about what he sees on the horizon. If that offends you, you are almost beyond saving, so take heart that you arrived just in the nick of time. The Ancient Hawaiians had a clear understanding of sexual energy as a force of creation and were simple and to the point in their portrayals of these understandings.

Referencing this frisky guy is the only way I have been able to denote the focal point energy that is the place for healing. Although it has been awkward at times, this single tiki has been my clue for unraveling thus far the mysteries of huna Magic that eluded even Max Freedom Long, the modern authority on huna. Thoughts of sex when one needs to get in touch with spirit may seem distasteful, but bear with me. After a good healing or mental housecleaning, the vigor and lust for life returns. So, basically what the ornery boy is saying is, "Look this way. It'll turn you on to the zest for life once more."

There, where the *pahoehoe* (smooth, granite-like, swirling lava) meets the ocean is the strongest focal point of energy for healing. A few moments in silence there and you will begin to realize that you have come to the Edge of Eternity and a doorway. For many this powerful energy of serenity will become the first true meaning of the word "church," beyond the boxes men have built to house God.

The Ritual of Healing and Forgiveness

Once you are near the water, ponder what it is that needs to be released in your life. Remember the basic wisdom for day-to-day living in Paradise. Never sleep under a coconut palm and never turn your back on the ocean. The tide is unpredictable here, even though you may find whatever happens to be significant and even symbolic to your experience. Many people seeking a cleansing have been "baptized" by an absolutely calm ocean. If you take your shoes off, be careful, because the lava surface is uneven.

Remember that the pure crystalline lava you are walking on is an "extension cord," a live conductor to the force of creation, Madam Pele, and, as ever, the foundation stone of new beginnings. Consider that within the lava is volcanic glass or obsidian, the "*Kahuna* Stone" and the "Mirror of the Soul." It will bring to the surface what needs to be healed. Be calm and take deep breaths. You are in a sanctuary that is the vortex for safely processing emotion and its built up residue, no matter how it may have manifested in your body or your life.

Allow *Honaunau* to be the perfect setting for you to get whatever point across to yourself that you need to understand, whatever has been an impasse or obstacle in your life.

Now consider this: Your journey has brought you to the sunset of your life over the sea of your creation. What is it that you would end this day forever? What is it that you would see through, absolve or clear up in your life? What has been holding you back? What has happened that you regret?

You may then ask it to be taken from you and to be filled with the understanding of its true meaning. Let go of anything that has diseased your thoughts and body, any thorn that has troubled your heart and any obstacle standing in the way of your magnificence. Don't worry about how real, finite or set in concrete the event, issue or circumstance may have seemed. You have come to the place where even the Earth liquefies. Don't be concerned if the situation seems impossible and beyond your reach. You have come to the place where spirit and the realm of possibility seems closer. For the moments that you are there you will feel you have left the old world behind and here, anything can happen (and does).

Give what you want to be rid of with each breath. The breath is an ancient *huna* "key" allowing the fantastic reservoir of your unconscious to do what it does best, just as your body knows how to replenish each cell and discard what it no longer needs, with every breath.

Your *unihipili* (unconscious mind) loves ritual and has the ability to bring the body back into balance. And so it is with trapped emotion, for your *unihipili* is in charge of your elaborate filing system of memories and has a direct link to that which runs your heartbeat, your *Aumakua,* your God-Link™.

As the sun disappears into the ocean and this day ends forever, turn *mauka* (towards the mountains) and witness the visual proof of the beauty and order of God which is our island Paradise. Say aloud *"Mahalo"* (thank you). One of the greatest oversights that has left dreams and prayers unfulfilled is the simple lack of closure. The unconscious mind will do its part in helping and making your deeper connection if you will remember to "declare it done!" Stating your intent out loud is important to the conscious, processing part of your mind. Believe that, due to your intention, it is done. Simply be *willing* (as discerned from willful) and it is done. The Angel Lady and miracle worker (see her section) tells us that those who receive healing are empowered by their very declaration and intent. Even the power of salvation from the highest authority of light can't get into your own personal situation until you give your permission and declaration that it is so. Do you realize the power that you have in saying no or even in "letting it slide?"

But will it last, you ask? Many have written months later telling of an even more real experience after leaving *Honaunau* and returning to their homes. During twilight sleep or meditation, they have found themselves standing on that lava again looking through the palms into the mountains, noticing the smell of the balmy air and other things they hadn't consciously experienced while they were actually there. The olfactory experience is a sign looked for in lucid dreaming that denotes an evolved level of consciousness has taken place. If a place has become more real in your dreams than it was when you physically experienced it you may ask yourself a wise old Hawaiian question. "Is my world an outpicturing of my thoughts?"

Never Miss a Hawaiian Sunset

Whether you are at *Honaunau* or not, the Western sides of the islands are the places for reflection. As with our American Indian brethren and my own tribe, the East and sunrise are always symbolic of the new day and another beginning. The West means completion and reflection, the looking within. As the crimson sun sets fire to the horizon each day in Paradise, it is a time to reflect upon your deeds and your destiny. Wherever you are, especially on the Kona side of the Big Island, be it driving through the rolling green hills of the Parker Ranch or at the Hilton for cocktails, stop for the moment that will etch another memory.

Wherever you travel throughout Paradise you will notice others doing the same. The ritual is automatic here, even for those time-clock punchers who had never noticed the sunsets of their old worlds. Most of the participants of the ritual are not metaphysical or esoteric thinkers but ordinary people, like you and I. Those who get the most out of this unsung ritual do share a few things in common; a little gray around the temples maybe, from having lived and experienced life to the point of appreciation to think enough to slow down and stop for a moment. These are the ones who have become part of the ancient ritual that they are not even aware of performing.

Although calming to the soul, it is impossible to witness a tropical Hawaiian sunset quietly. Here, the small white globe you have always taken for granted suddenly balloons out over the ocean. By 6 PM it is a mammoth orange pumpkin, overpowering the landscape. You stop what you are doing. Within a few moments of wordless silence, the inner floodgates of your mind begin to ponder everything you hold sacred. Automatically the display of fiery beauty lifts you out of the mundane, reminding you of a bigger picture. A thought comes to you. This ritual has gone on since the beginning of time. The next thought. It will continue long after your story is over . . . long after all the world's problems have disappeared. Earthly concerns vaporize, but you feel mortal. For a moment there is another lump in the throat. It seems as though your life to now has passed like a rush of water under the bridge. A sense of urgency subsides. Within the temple of your thoughts the sacred book, known only to you . . . your book, falls open once again. You reflect upon loved ones and the things that might have been. There is a tug at your heart for something that you wish you could have changed. Years pass in an eternal moment. The sun is crimson now, filling your entire reality. Then, at the bottom of your thoughts, you discover an ember, a half-forgotten dream. Your chest feels the deep breath it hasn't known for quite a while. You are one with the enormity of the sun, igniting the ember for one more time, giving you back the fuel your soul so deeply craves. The sun of another day, like none that has come before, like none that ever will be again, sinks quietly into the horizon. A part of you realizes. It leaves a personal painting just for you, a painting of passion in the clouds. The easel of Heaven fades into night, on the Rembrandt that never will be again.

You have experienced a Hawaiian sunset.

If you have evolved spiritually (beyond the orthodoxy of religion) you will connect with this understanding. If you need to release something, this then is the time to perform the earlier ritual of *Honaunau*. Barefoot on the lava or the sand is just so much the better. Sometimes the full body/mind immersion can be achieved by simply leaning against the car door or loosening a tie. As the Hawaiians say, it is only the thought that counts.

Use your breath and let your body do the rest. It knows how to release everything it no longer needs, beyond the cellular level.

Dreams of a shack on the beach or a coffee shack on the mountain? That's just your Paradise within, calling you. Remember, you'll never really own it until it's a feeling inside.

Things that you regret? Just let it all go . . . and ask . . . out loud. It'll do you good—sometimes beyond your expectations.

And by the way, the sun sets elsewhere, most everywhere you are likely to be.

The Legend of the Green Flash

"All came from the Dreamtime, the source of all reality. Nothing would be in the world unless it were first dreamed of. The Dreamers are those who lead the way. They are closer to the Maker. They lift us from the place of suffering and hopelessness, transforming the ordinary earthly experience into a playground of the Divine."

If you are lucky—and Hawaii is the home office for luck—you'll witness a green flash when the sun hits the water. National Geographic spent a bundle trying to capture it on film and finally captured a tiny bit of it. Depending upon the time of year, it can be a spectacular little occurrence.

Sometimes it flashes when the sun touches the ocean but often it's just as it disappears. Occasionally the green flash will shoot towards you but most experience it as a lime green laser exploding outwards across the horizon.

Legend has it that this is another doorway opening—one that may have been unapproachable before. This is the Earth Mother revealing her heart to you and it has to do with your prosperity, your richness of the life experience.

In the ancient wisdom of the Eastern tradition, green is a color of the heart *chakra,* which is the vibration of chlorophyll and that which sustains life on our planet.

The green frequency is the frequency of abundance like crops yield at harvest. It is interesting to note that countries with the most stable economies adorn their currency with this color.

So, like the ritual of Madame Pele and the force of creation, what is it that you would wish for, now that you have traveled all this way? Now that the door may finally be open.

Unlike the seriousness of the journey to volcano and the doorway to creation, this notion often gives a lucky feeling and the desire to dare to dream again. This may be the door you have been knocking on for quite a while.

Nine

Heiaus:
Sacred Spots

As we continue this journey and look at what I call "The first people, the first teaching" I am reminded of another Hawaiian proverb: "The path to God is a simple one of Joy." In fact, it is not a path at all. What starts as an outward search always ends up as an uncovering of something that existed within us all along. Something, the elders would say, that may have been forgotten from time to time along the journey of life, which can happen with children who become sleepy or whose attention tends to wander now and then.

Through my own personal experiences and intuition I have come to believe that the profound wisdom of the Ancient Hawaiians (before *kapu*) was based on an intuitive higher connection instead of a conscious, intellectual knowing. This connection was strongest during a time when women were equal and the Hawaiians were semi-nomadic and were "drawn to" move around to certain places on the islands. The later knowing based upon the *kapu* system is but a remnant of the original knowledge, and was often used in manipulation of power as an exercise of the will. Both of these two distinct divisions of knowledge have been called the science of *huna* (Essence of the life force), but I believe the latter to be a distortion and a coverup. This coverup appears to have happened with the similar wisdom of all tribal (indigenous) peoples around the world, having to do with an attitude towards the opposite sex and an unwillingness to be led and not "rooted down." In Hawaii the earlier science was a religious way of life and possibly the first teaching on our planet. The second, more familiar remnant in modern times could be better categorized as low-grade witchcraft.

The Hawaiian *kahunas* (original stewards of the essence) had the ability to intuitively identify centers of a certain concentrated energy force and when they were active. Some of these energy centers are still marked by ruins that you will see throughout the islands. Unfortunately the real ones are mixed in with *kapu* locations that were selected through unenlighted will, as a man would select a building site for a house based only upon its view. Some energy centers are surrounded by rock walls, usually with a square rock mantle or platform at its center. All are known as Hawaiian *heiaus* (sacred spots). The word *heiau* (hey ee ow) itself has a *kapu* (forbidden) quality about it that should be reevaluated, as should the entire body of knowledge called *huna,* in order to clarify and reclaim the earlier, more powerful and deeper understanding. Today *heiau* means a sacred place of worship. Both the words sacred and worship automatically bring to mind the connotation of something *kapu* or forbidden. *Heiaus* were indeed always places of worship, but at one time that simply meant a place of higher focus and quiet thought, without the forbidden connotation. Perhaps the overtones came through centuries of children telling children not to play there because it is hard to concentrate when something else is going on. I don't know for sure, but I think that is probably what happened in a lot of areas where there is dark energy or misunderstandings today, because the literal meaning of *heiau* does not mean to worship in our traditional sense. *Heiau* means a place where one can "capture a current of energy."

Just as the energy is different in a quiet park under a palm tree than, let's say, on the L.A. freeway at rush hour, the energy in various spots on the Big Island is identifiably different. The early *kahunas* were sensitive to these energy differences and could categorize them. There were places to tap into the current for the weather of a certain area, called *heiau ka lua ua.* These energy centers were used for asking for the rain to be turned on or off, and even changing (baking) the elements of weather, having to do with clouds and air currents. Could this be coincidental to the rainmakers of American Indian tribes and the popular sideshow rainmakers of our early 20th century America? Perhaps even the charlatans were intuiting a higher possible connection. After all, out of that came the later seeding of clouds for rain.

There were sacred places where the *kahuna* would tap into the current for healing the physical or emotional body, called *heiau ho ola,* to balance the current of the body by purging the vibration (by a kind of gurgling, shaking or tempering). Because everything was considered to be formed from vibration, the *kahuna* would chant the sound that cooperated with the current and then direct it differently.

There were even places where the current for good fishing could be tapped into, *heiau ho'o ulu i'a* (to call upon the bowl of energy that is the center frequency attention of swarming fish and to intensify and move it to be the bowl (center catchment) of my net). Have you ever been snorkeling or scuba diving in a swarm of fish? It looks as though an invisible magnet is in the center moving them to change direction. Could the ancient Hawaiians have been aware of this sophisticated invisible intrinsic factor, this homing device energy? They described its properties and resonance as spherical and similar to the clapper of a bell or a bowling ball. In an understanding that still eludes modern physics, the *kahuna* knew this energy could be evoked and directed much like sonar and had a snowballing, reverberating wavelength that could be intensified. A wavelength that was on the frequency of the life forces that respond to swarming.

There are stories to this day of "Auntie" singing a love song to the fishes while wading. The tale goes that when she held her apron up in a bowl, the fishes that would want to be dinner would jump out of the water into her apron. I have heard these stories from many *kahunas.*

Indeed, it is my far-out contention, through a new look at the Hawaiian chant, that the Ancient Ones could astral-travel from vortex to vortex (*heiau* to *heiau*), knowing when certain star alignments would "open the doors," so to speak. There is nothing to substantiate this of course, but it would begin to explain the cross-knowledge of tribes around the world who have never met.

If you visit *heiaus* please stay off them and disturb nothing. Instead try this: Be still and notice whether the energy there is of a troubled or a calm nature. You will be surprised at how easy it is to identify the difference. You may then become aware of whether it is a *heiau* for healing or not. If the energy feels supportive and soothing, you may choose to meditate further. Remember that the Big Island is the island that has awakened and you are standing at the doorway to other realities; therefore other possibilities may happen. So, if you need a miracle, go ahead and expect one.

Human Sacrifice

One of the most intense clairvoyant experiences I have had on this island had to do with the *heiaus* used for human sacrifice. There are not as many of these places as some may think. Some believe that Pele's anger, expressed in her outpouring of lava, is purging the *heiaus* that were used for human sacrifice near her current flow on the southeastern side of the Big Island.

Of the three times I have encountered the mysterious *kahuna* underground movement, this subject and my views on *kapu* have aroused the most controversy. To claim back their pride and joy and help a world in its time of need, the Hawaiian people must discern the truth of the old ways and purge the misunderstandings that have occurred, the worst of which was human sacrifice. The Hawaiians had no edge on the market when it came to the unspeakable. Having been involved in human sacrifice as a paid killer financed by your tax dollars in Vietnam, I am qualified to give an opinion on the subject. Since most of my readers are American taxpayers, I ask that you suspend judgment on the Hawaiian people for any acts they may have committed in the distant past. The fact is that most cultures have supported "the act" at one time or another in their evolution. It is one of the great enigmas of the Human Race.

Somewhere between the Eastern concept of reincarnation and the Hawaiian/American Indian understanding of ancestry is a way of remembering the part of us that has lived forever. It has to do with ego-association. It is clear in my head—it just won't roll off my tongue by press time. Anyway, asking your full indulgence, it is important that you at least consider my story from the viewpoint of a past-life experience to maintain a larger perspective on this very shocking experience I am about to share. As modern psychology contends, no matter what our conscious beliefs, our subconscious minds believe in past lives. That is the only way I can explain some of the information that has come through and my vivid clairvoyant and clairaudient experiences in the islands.

I have sensed the negative energy where human sacrifice may have occurred in several places on the Big Island. One is within a master *heiau* known as *Umi* at the top of *Hualalai* Mountain (curiosity seekers forget the trek—it is easier to go try and walk on the moon). Even though the middle of the *Umi* grid can give you "crocodile skin" (as Uncle George terms it), it is important to note that the decadent practices prevailed only for a brief time during a lengthy history.

After visiting *Umi* I chose to cleanse and reactivate a grid within this *heiau* with my own ritual blessing. If this offends some Hawaiians, *i kala mai i a'u.* I must always do what is with my *na'au.* Since it is a focal point of energy on a grid that effects my home in Kona and my "church" at *Honaunau,* I found that I had no choice but to make the pilgrimage.

Shortly thereafter, on a speaking panel with a Hawaiian University Professor, I received a confirmation of *Umi's* alignment.

What I'm leading up to with this discussion of alignments is that, from a metaphysical point of view, the energy of certain places remains active throughout time. Because of this these places should be "clarified" ritualistically for higher intent of this force to prevail, just as you bless the sticks and stones of a new house to let your energy prevail until it becomes a home.

A good example of how this energy may continue throughout centuries is Tienamin Square in China where the student protest startled the last great stronghold of communism and the media worldwide. The free world will never forget that young man who singlehandedly fended off a tank in front of global news cameras. It cost him his life, as well as an untold number of other lives.

The point I am making is that this *"heiau* for human sacrifice" is still active with the same energy, even after centuries. Would this have been helpful input to the students looking for picnic spots to protest upon? Remember the analogy of the park setting and the L.A. freeway. The energy is different and you are less likely to have a car wreck in the middle of your picnic if it is in the park. So it is with the different energy of *heiaus.*

The shocker came for me at the *Mo'okini heiau* next to the birthplace of Hawaii's greatest king, at the north end of the island. As I said, not all the energy is black and this place has had other uses. But this *heiau* and *Pu'u kohola heiau* near Spencer Beach have the same sinister effect on me. I get the same predominantly abusive dark male energy at one of the small *heiaus* behind the Kona Lagoon Hotel and in a few caves that I have entered.

It was a blustery day with high winds at the *heiau* near King Kamehameha's birthplace. *Maui's* famous *Haleakala* crater was clearly visible on the horizon. I entered the *Mo'okini heiau,* and immediately got "pictures" of a wedding ceremony in full regalia.

As I walked and stood in certain places, the pictures flooded my mind and seemed to be of different times in history. This part of the experience was pleasant, like returning to one's old home or birthplace, or the foundations where a home once stood, and recalling memories of what went on there. Then, it suddenly happened.

I put my hand on one of several large hollowed lava stones and the visions started rolling. I could see everything about as clearly as if a shard of sunlight had come through a smoke-filled barroom. It was as real and horrifying as anything I had ever witnessed—and I had seen men blown apart on the battlefield.

It appeared as though I were standing in the middle of a grueling ritual of human sacrifice. Frozen in terror, all I could do was witness it. I felt that if I moved, I would be seen, as though I was standing smack in the middle of what was happening.

The men were huge. They seemed seven feet tall. Two were holding a boy down while a third, evidently the priest, committed the unspeakable act.

Directly in front of the proceedings the next sacrifice, a very horrified young man, was forced to watch. I thought I had seen it all in combat but the frenzied and despicable sexual overtones promptly made me vomit, releasing the stone and (thank God) interrupting my connection with the proceedings. I was immediately snapped back into the 20th century with a messed up T-shirt.

I have not heard from the person who accompanied me on my sightseeing tour since that day. I am sure she would rather visit places that are just a bunch of rocks with normal people who don't cause public embarrassments.

Through this "memory activation," the significance of which I relate to my Vietnam combat experiences and my reason for teaching, I have come to understand full well the suppressed, latent, homoerotic sexual energy that is the misuse of control at the highest levels of power throughout history. This denial energy is precisely what Hitler used to mold his SS and run his dynasty in fear.

This misuse of the *kundalini* is Mankind's furthest fall from grace in defiance of the light and love of God. One would be even more shocked at the incredible number of charismatic leaders throughout time and to this day who have studied and harnessed sexual energy through tantric practices.

I am not against tantric sex, only the misuse of it. I am, however, not liberal in this area and contend that most of these practices are misused for charisma and manipulation.

Throughout history, more women than meet the eye have also been forced to use this energy for survival or to get what they think they want.

I am expounding on sex here because it is one of the most important issues for the human race, which thinks that they were conceived in sin, to understand. A total rethinking of our identity in this area is necessary for our next evolutionary step.

The Hawaiians have a natural understanding in this area which was originally connected to *huna.* Through a guilt trip laid on them by the missionaries, it is also what cost them everything—land, religion, identity and most of their race.

Since my experience at the sacrificial area of this *heiau* I have developed my theory on the core-level guilt that would cause a race to experience genocide, as my tribe the Cherokee did in the events surrounding our own holocaust in Oklahoma, known as the Trail of Tears.

To fathom how this could happen to innocent people, the reader will have to consider the term *karma* and entertain a concept of a higher order and the notion that all things may make sense in a larger context. Most Hawaiians no longer carry this guilt, which is easily abolished therapeutically through their own recently rediscovered methods, now made popular in neurolinguistic programming.

The few "bad seed" *kahunas* that I have encountered who still abuse this power suffer from a "castration complex" of resentment that still remains from the missionary onslaught. This complex is often blamed for the high percentage of "gay" Hawaiians, which is absolutely not so. Contrary to popular misconception, "gay" is not a mental disorder (see Temple of Woman in the next section for more detail).

Suffice it to say the Hawaiians never had any real edge on the market when it came to abuse of power. This has happened from the time man climbed down from the treetops.

Perhaps, in this defining moment in all history, we can begin to look at the dark side of human nature and learn from our mistakes, starting with the suppression of our sexuality. The ancient ones knew that the balance of this energy was considered the very life-force of the Universe, the *Ai,* the coming together and *Aina,* the expression or manifestation, which is the land that is the product of *Pele,* the Earth itself.

The Sacred Temple of Woman

Before *kapu* and the control of women, before woman was made the property of man, all women shared a direct connection with the force of creation known now as *Pele.*

This connection was denied all but the "special people," the people who bridged the sexes.

Today, referred to as "gay," these people maintained the harmony between the polarity of men and women and were considered the joy of each. They intervened whenever things got too serious, balancing everything in the community, including the population itself. They naturally mirrored to each sex its other side.

All her sisters knew Pele's temperament, for it was their own. They knew when she would flow, for it had to do with their flow.

The clue to this sacred connection was their menstrual cycle. Knowing that this was a special time of vulnerability and the "mood" of the goddess, men respected it.

During this special time of the month, women were not required to work and were waited on by men just as if they were with child. Then man listened to woman for any messages from Pele and all was harmonious in the Garden.

Pele, *Wahine Kapu,* the unknowable woman, and her sisters of the night represented a connection with God that was not controllable or manipulable by man. This was the time before respect turned into fear, when the night brought reflection and the joy of the *night rainbow* which was the connection with the living ancestors. (See the "First People, First Teaching" section.) This was the time before *kapu* and the denial rules formed by man that spread hopelessness and separation throughout the planet.

This was the time before *his* story. This was the time of no illness, when there was but one rule to live by—a Golden Rule.

The Vagina Cave

The feminine archetype of creation, Pele, recently revealed herself on the Hilo side of the Big Island. In the jungle near a small, rustic resort called *Kalanihonua,* is the mysterious Vagina Cave. It is anatomically correct, about six feet overall, illuminated eerily at certain times by sunlight shining through the roof of the cave. It is said to have been a mystical healing experience for all who were fortunate to go there before the State of Hawaii recently closed it down. It is a shame that because of a sad few and their bureaucratic nonsense, sacred sites such as this one have become forbidden to all.

Ten

The
Paranormal

Mysterious Saddle Road

I have suggested the lava tube experience to completely divorce yourself from the 20th century world and get you into a higher mind set and dilated state of awareness. Two other escapades will help instigate this for you, providing a foundation for the experience of a lifetime. One is the simple trip around an island in a rental car. Too many people spend their entire vacation in the confines of a single resort. The mega-resorts are designed that way to satisfy all physical desires so that folks won't wander away with some of their mega-bucks. They are built on the Disneyland theme, geared for adults, with boutique and cocktail pit stops instead of ice cream and ferris wheels. Because of lazy human nature, most folks settle for familiar comfort wherever they go. Same air-conditioned hotel room as home, same McDonald's burger.

Do yourself a favor and step into another world by first getting out, getting alone and thereby getting in touch with it. Stop at the local gas station shacks and roadside stands for a snack instead of the tourist traps. Like a rustic old painting, they proudly display their paint-peeled names of their Japanese-Hawaiian heritage. Vine-ripened fruit is always available to awaken the gustatory and olfactory senses out of your old world and into the greater dimension.

Pull over to the side of the road for no reason and walk off into the bush (especially at sunset). Just obey your horse sense and realize that nothing can kill you in Paradise. There aren't even any snakes.

Only a few islands can be circumnavigated, *Oahu*, the Big Island and now *Maui*, but the one-day trek will hold an entirely new experience for you even if you have to double back over the same road. Remember that life itself is a journey, not a destination. The only good of having a destination is to give momentum and focus to getting the wheels of our lives turning, otherwise we stagnate. The folks who really connect, peel away from the crowd and the preconceived game plan, and go with the flow and simply "experience."

Another great escapade, although a slightly forbidden one is the Saddle Road journey. It is a paved but windy, bumpy trail up into the mountains, bisecting the island. Like going to another planet, it is a strange, unique journey within itself and the better part of a day should be set aside. It is nestled between Mauna Loa and Mauna Kea, two of the three major mountains that make up the island. It stretches from the rolling green hills of the Parker Ranch in Waimea on the Kona Airport side, to the wet rainforests of Hilo. The bad news is that car rental agencies forbid you to drive there.

Some of the rental agencies were supposed to have given in to protest, hopefully by the press time of this extended edition of the book. Although it is a winding road full of potholes, Saddle Road is an expressway compared to some of the roads allowed for rental use on other islands. The road to Hana on nearby Maui is an example where rental cars are allowed and shouldn't be. I lost all four hub caps and damn near had a head-on collision at every turn on that "tank proving ground." The question then arises: Why is tourism discouraged up on Saddle Road? And why all the hoopla surrounding the big Army base at the top of Saddle Road? Just try meandering off the main road and all of sudden you have an escort of a couple of good ol' boys in a pick-up truck. Their blue jeans might pass unnoticed if it weren't for their Army boot-camp haircuts.

A retired naval officer who has watched the base being built since World War II, claims he has seen many strange things being transported up the mountain, including nuclear silos and enough materials to build an underground city. And what about that partially covered airstrip big enough for a 747?

Saddle Road is indeed a place of strange new and old phenomenon. The UFO activity is so commonplace there that it is no longer denied, including three nights in a recent month which made the papers and local radio. Low-flying blue lights coming from Maui were spotted flying in between the mountains and then hanging a left. It was denied by the military base on radio by insinuating that a new weapon was being fired. Then a caller said, "So your new weapon hangs a left, huh, Colonel?" It was then confessed that the military didn't know what the source of the strange blue lights could have been. A fun thing that many of us have done is tricking the guards up at the military installation. Whenever we encountered a guard we would casually comment on last night's UFO activity. Once they acknowledged "Yeah, they were flying through here like Dallas International." After a few of these tricks, no one to my knowledge has been allowed contact with the guards since.

Other mysteries surrounding Saddle Road stem from Hawaiian Legend and I don't know the UFO connection yet, but since the new data on the monuments of Mars, the two worlds seem to be coming closer together. My teaching slogan is "A key to our future lies in the past." Somehow the afterlife, the before life, and now are interconnected. The veil is being lifted, and the Big Island is the place where worlds collide, so I expect major information breakthroughs soon.

It is a fact that something or some force had destroyed every attempt to put a good highway through Saddle Road. The locals say that Madame Pele wouldn't allow it. And then, there were the sightings of the Night Marchers, the seven-foot-tall ghosts of Hawaiian guards carrying torches. Since the first printing of this book Saddle Road was finally successfully "paved" for the most part. A "spaceport" freeway now spans much of it, while the spooky feeling still prevails to this day with continued, unexplained phenomena.

When you venture up there, you will find that it is eerie and beautiful, like taking the first trek to Venus. With a four-wheel-drive vehicle, you can go up the Mauna Kea road to the observatories at its summit. There you will find many telescopes, including the world's largest reflective telescope, a six-nation participation. This is the only place in the world where you can snow ski and still make it back to snorkel at the beach before sunset. Watch out for fog and "spooks" on Saddle Road and whatever your government dollars are up to. If it doesn't disturb your gut and you don't get caught, stop and "tune in" for a while. You will feel as though you have established a radio antenna on top of the farthest outpost.

The Night Marchers

Depending upon your attitude, some encounters can be a little hair-raising on the Big Island. You had better be centered with a good grip on joy if you encounter these characters, who are said to be disincarnate spirits or *unihipili*. This is sometimes a negative connotation but can also be the Hawaiian description of the unconscious mind. It is the soul-force that is immortal and the bridge between worlds. The current trend of serious exploration into the paranormal would achieve monumental understanding if researchers would look at things from the Hawaiian viewpoint. The decadence of *huna* in its *kapu* era used witchcraft to entrap and manipulate the souls of the departed. The simple understanding was that a soul in transition without its conscious mind, ego-identification could be manipulated while it was confused. This sounds familiar to what we are learning about haunted houses and the lost souls that hang around forever walking the same stairs and such. The Night Marchers often appear as the giant guards of the *Ali i* (Royalty) bearing torches and wearing face paint. Sometimes drums can be heard accompanying their marches on Saddle Road or the golf courses near the Kona Gold Coast mega-resorts as well as at other nearby sacred sites and trails on the northwestern side of the island.

It is said that if one of these seven- or eight-foot warriors should suddenly appear, scaring the hell out of you, it is appropriate to turn your head away, avoid eye contact and bow.

There is an evolved process of handling this very enlightening encounter that I will not go into at this point. Suffice it to say that all encounters on this island should be approached with respect for the myriad things that one may not be aware of that go on within these places of unusual energy phenomena.

Depending upon where you are coming from, sometimes the magic isn't all that white. This is the island that has awakened and, although it is Paradise, it is not the easiest island to live on, particularly if a person is harboring fear. But, if you will know yourself and brave another dimension of thinking, everything will come out all right and you will join the ranks of the next pioneers, those who would pierce the veil of the ordinary and delve into the excitement of an entirely new realm. Or is it new?

UFO Activity

"What does the new have to do with the old? Have we come this way before? There is something strangely familiar about it all."

UFO activity is peskiest through Saddle Road, Oceanview and South Point on the Big Island. They like *Waimea* Canyon on *Kau'ai* and *Haleakula Crater* in *Maui* also. For that matter so will you, but I believe the main "doorway," as it were, is the Big Island—for reasons that may seem almost logical to you now. From my years in the military I would say that there is an apparent government cover-up and/or collaboration going on of some sort. The trouble is the government is not bright enough to conspire. If you have ever worked for any branch of it you know it can't find its butt with a flashlight and both hands. However, when I was Chief of Military Police at Camp Pendelton, I was responsible for stationing Marine guards at top secret installations worldwide. The stories that filtered back still prickle the hair on the back of my neck. The men who think they are in charge of secrets may not be bright enough to conspire, but boys will be boys and somebody is really screwing around with things that are not public knowledge.

As a friend of mine who is a famous astronaut would tell

you, "Anyone who isn't aware of UFO existence is not living in the 20th century."

What may be interesting to note about "close encounters" is that they claim to be of two separate origins. The one of interest to our own origin may have to do with a star in the Pleiades. The others, reported to be insect-like, are apparently cold-blooded jerks, an infestation that we may have brought upon ourselves and now cannot get rid of.

The most famous proven case in regard to the good guys from the Pleiades is the Billy Meier series of encounters in Switzerland. I had a close personal friend from Universal Studios connected with the investigation of this case. His friend, who pioneered the research, is retired military and one of the world's foremost experts on UFOs. This case involved over 700 computer-enhanced photographs. There were two limited-edition volumes issued containing these photos, which have not successfully been disputed even after many thousands of people have seen them.

I do not mention the latter gentleman's name because he has since been sent to Arizona Federal Penitentiary for an unspeakable crime that we know he didn't commit. His incarceration occurred at the same time that he was researching a UFO government coverup case in the Arizona/Nevada desert.

My friend tells me that the gentleman is happy to be alive and was warned not to investigate further. Incidentally, the man was in Tucson the day the offense he was charged with was said to have occurred in Phoenix.

The reason I have mentioned all of this is because of the fascinating ancient Hawaiian connection. This involves many books out on the Hawaiian market, such as *Tales From The Night Rainbow* from the island of *Moloka'i*. These sources claim that the original inhabitants of these islands, before Polynesian control, were the first folks on this planet, seeded from another galaxy. The chants claim to be

26,000 years old and talk about the time when the islands of Hawaii were called *Mu* or *LeMuria*. The thing that thrills me the most are the connections to the myths and legends we have told our children for centuries. My predictions have a high accuracy and I really stuck my neck out in the 1970s. I said 1995 would be the first disclosure proof of alien existence nationwide, and by the turn of the century they would come to dinner.

The myths all fit together somehow with the Egyptian extraterrestrial gods and similar tribal myths around the world. The whole story will probably soon be made public, complicating everyone's lives and screwing up their religious beliefs. And just as you are beginning to have fun and find it interesting here, you're liable to be abducted. And so we had all better knock off the seriousness and prepare to enjoy the ride. It is all rather bizarre, but sure is getting interesting. I hope it will be fun—after all, that is what the new dimension of life should be all about.

 # Eleven

Friends from Forever

The Dolphin Experience

"Brothers and sisters of the watery realm. To remind us of our beauty, freedom and innocence. To help in the transition. To heal the sorrow and the severed connection. To bridge the worlds. To claim back love and joy. To find our way home."

The reconnection with nature is a must for every soul during a time of great change. Being Paradise, Hawaii provides the very essence of this, plus the ability to process and see through the illusion of whatever corner we may have painted ourselves into in life. Hawaii is the highest mountain to stand on the most remote escape and the deepest mirror to look into in putting our lives back into perspective. I believe that we have been given brothers and sisters to help us in this reconnection process.

My own sacred encounter with the dolphins happened when I had found my way home to Hawaii out of the world of finance. I was at the end of one of my ropes and feeling lonely after having abandoned the games of love and life. Those ropes had become shorter and flimsier but still had many strings attached. I had been processing heavy emotions after saying goodbye to my only means of income, a little crystal shop in Kona. The emotional ties were a knot called Christa, the mate of soul, if there is such a thing. My return to Hawaii had meant that our ships had finally passed in the night, a departure of eleven years.

Nothing had worked for me since Vietnam. I was in my 40s and was worn out trying to figure out what I wanted to be when I grew up. So I took up snorkeling. Over the months this filled my social activities to the point of encompassing something I hadn't addressed in years—church. I had got to where I could hold my breath down to 85 feet in meditation and had met a few new friends.

One recent acquaintance was connected with a remaining fear. He was a moray eel, the biggest I had ever heard about, with a girth the size of my leg. The closest I had got back to God before that time was a turtle ride, which (of course) was now a $5,000 fine. That figured, because my only other semblance of church was the *Honaunau,* City of Refuge, which had just begun charging an entry fee.

The female owner of the scuba locker boasted of night rides on 12-foot manta rays, which would stir any vagabond's soul. Unfortunately, at the time all I thought about riding was her. I had never seen a more shapely wet suit. This time the thought of a one-night stand only brought a deeper look into the mirror and all I saw was a receding hairline. I was at that awkward age for a man where hormones propelled by alcohol could no longer cover a broken heart.

And so, putting my lust and the everyday world aside, I would free dive deeper each day, looking for what I didn't have a clue. On occasion I visited my sinister friend, Lucifer, the eel, always keeping a respectful distance. When I look back on it all now I realize I must have had a suicide wish, considering what happened next.

One of the diversions keeping me from facing my life was a legacy I brought back from the war. Despite hundreds of night patrols in the Vietnam jungle I still had fears in my life. Stupid little fears that I had gone on a campaign about since moving to Hawaii. After all, how could a guy live in Paradise if he were still afraid of centipedes? Wishing to face all my fears of life, I had already got more than I bargained for in lessons from the night-side and *Wahine Kapu,* Madame Pele. Encounters in the death caves and a few evenings on Saddle Road had filled the bill and scared my pants off. Still there was this mortal feeling I despised, whenever I encountered something I couldn't control. I didn't know it was a diversion and an excuse for not living.

It was another day in Paradise at *Ho okena,* a secluded beach south of my sleepy village of Kona. Up until then the closest my dolphin friends had come while I was snorkeling was within 100 yards or so. In meditation I had zeroed in on what did and did not attract them. They seemed to come around only after I had taken my mind completely off them and only when I was experiencing, what I called the slight "joy of the moment." The Hawaiians called it "now time," the doorway to real living. Any moment out of the now where scheming or a thought of pretense came into my mind and zoom, they were out of there. Even these closer encounters with the dolphins were rare and usually came after an hour of trying to mimic their sounds, while spinning and flopping around in the water with the total abandonment of a yahoo.

This day at the lagoon I was feeling old and defeated by life, so I had given up on the little fuckers. I distinctly remember the prelude to what was about to happen. It was just after carving my heart out over Christa for the last time. My memories of the shambles of my life lay bleeding on the beach all around me. It had been another day in Paradise as all days, except for a feeling that something was finally over with. A cherished memory flashed Christa's face to me like a painting. A painting that had somehow captured and revealed to me a part of her I had never noticed nor fully appreciated. It was a moment of precious realism I can only compare to what must happen in the sobering days that follow the loss of a child. For a stark moment, she was all women, all love, beyond the games we had played around love. At that moment the picture was pulled away from me, as if a book, holding precious secrets that I had only glimpsed, was closing forever.

I was left in the middle of an unannounced funeral saying goodbye out loud. Out squeaked the voice of a five-year-old. Suddenly, the island I was standing on seemed as if it shrank to the size of a charcoal briquette. My reality was nothing without love. My love was nothing but a memory. That memory was nothing but an illusion. My life had become a clinging to what was no longer. I was totally alone in the Universe. The quiet thunderclap of realization was devastating.

The wind blew through me and I was hollow as I entered the water. My call home to Hawaii had been a series of these initiations, each one severing another tie to my old life. And now, even the comfort found in the pain of memory was being torn away. Just as the day I returned stateside, hollow from Vietnam, I was being emptied out again.

I floated above Lucifer's home in the coral. Still stunned and indifferent I took a shallow dive to see if the devil was in. There he was, coiled and looking 10 feet longer than normal and as thick as Schwarzenegger's leg. The strange enticement found in fear focused me in the now, camouflaging the pain of my soul. If only I hadn't seen that diver getchi-gooing moray eels on "National Geographic" last week, I wouldn't have been challenged to do something stupid. And it did have to be a girl diver at that.

There he was, staring up, mouth and gills billowing at me like a fire-breathing dragon of folklore and legend. I had only touched the small eels before now, mostly by accident with a quick "whew" and an unspoken thankfulness for having got away with it. Even after combat I was still chicken when it came to some of the littler things in life, the creepy crawlies, the creatures. I knew if he latched on that would be it. A python that large was trouble enough. But one wrapped in a coral reef in 40 feet of water was certain to be fatal.

In a few days I could be a cadaver on the beach with a chunk out of its arm. The strangest things always crossed my mind when I was at a crossroads. Gray hair and not enough of it in the right places, I said to myself, feeling old, very, very old. The flame of the warrior dwindled. The ex-Marine was on his last patrol.

I floated back to the surface and started my *huna* breathing. I lay motionless in the water, thinking only of my bald spot, which was probably getting sunburned. Shit!

The last thing I remember was looking at the tears in my mask over Christa while the feeling of total indifference crept over me like rigor mortis. Two more deep breaths and then I would go.

Just then it happened. I was swept up almost out of the water by an incredible, slick black swirling force. This was accompanied by a deafening chatter that ended almost as instantaneously as it had begun. My breath, which had completely left me in fear, became the deepest inhalation of pure joy I had ever experienced. Seven dolphins darted away in all directions. One took a final pass and brushed me, yapping excitedly as if to say something. The message bombarded my startled consciousness. "Lighten up!!" I gasped. I sputtered. I uttered half-sentences, not knowing what to say, how to react. Finally I laughed aloud. I sat on the beach for what must have been an hour of stunned gratitude.

After doing cart wheels back into town I just had to share my experience and brag a little. "The dolphins saved me," I declared. "They swept me out of the water, just when I had given up hope!" Overhearing me, an old salt at meditation popped my ego bubble before it had a chance to form.

"That's nothing," he said smugly. "There is a gal down there that rides them. She just whistles and chirps whenever she's swimming and they all come around."

I have never met this lady. But I believe the tale, even though these are considered the wild, little, untrainable Pacific dolphins. That day they not only answered a call for help that I didn't know I was shouting, they bridged a world I had only read about in Grandmother Twila's animal cards. A world I had only dreamt of in my talks with my Indian grandfather, a world I had hoped existed but never knew. To this day I continue to learn from that brief moment in eternity. Yes, they probably saved a life that day, but more importantly they put one back on the path. And they gave an ordinary guy his first true religious experience. One he had been looking for all his life in the boxes that men built for God. One that he hopes to share someday with his grandchildren and anybody who feels that they have lost their connection. A religious experience that an old veteran who was disillusioned with life will never forget. Thanks, guys. I quit eating tuna.

The only thing that comes close to the dolphin experience is a whale watch encounter. I can only describe it as brushing up next to a living, moving skyscraper-building full of love. It is a wonderful ritual that can be participated in off the Kona Coast of the Big Island and *Maui* yearly, but that is another story in Paradise.

The Angel Connection

"We are near the end. The end of a long nightmare. Someone is there in the dark. Could it be that I have never been alone?"

Many Alaskan pioneers have been drawn to the Big Island of Hawaii as a last frontier.

One of the most beautiful souls in my life is one of these pioneers known in the islands as the "Angel Lady," Miriam Baker. Now an octogenarian, Miriam is one of the youngest hearts and oldest souls I have ever met. In Alaska she owned a trucking business of 18-wheelers and Caterpillar tractors. Our first encounter was a brief one when I opened a little crystal shop after returning to the Big Island in the early 1980s.

One day she thundered up over the curb in her Oldsmobile and onto the sidewalk, flung the trunk open and carried in her books to sell. I liked her instantly and felt a powerful connection, but it would be years before we worked together. Now that I look back on it, I suppose I needed to first have a few encounters like that of the dolphins, to prepare me for her special magic.

Miriam has been working with Angels for over 50 years and her miracles in manifesting are known in the private sector the world over. She has influenced the highest levels of government, which was the recent topic of controversial AP and UPI interviews. She was psychically called to the island as were many other special people of a worldwide gathering that has been taking place there. To date over 140 of these souls have returned to Hawaii with the same vision of healing centers and a new thought university that I had in a near-death experience while in combat in Vietnam.

Ms. Baker was initiated into the secret order of the Essene under Florida State charter over half a century ago. This was contemporaneous with the first spiritual wave of great thinking called the "I Am" movement of the 1930s and the great depression. Out of this time came most of the first wave of monumental thinkers of this century and probably the very foundation stones for anything that could now be termed "New Age."

The Essenes have remained a secret order throughout time, going public only since the discovery of the Dead Sea Scrolls. Miriam was told over 30 years ago that these scrolls would be found and was sworn to secrecy concerning certain wisdom until this occurrence. Jesus was said to have been a rebel priest of this order. It is considered one of the three original teachings of our planet, the Theraputi, or therapist approach to life, the Maggi, or magicians, and the Essene, those closest to the Hawaiians, people of the spirit or "essence" of life.

Ms. Baker channels an entity of the Brotherhood known as "Adono." She is the author of three books, the most important of which is *Our Angels And Our Mysteries.* She has identified the qualities of the angelic realm rather differently than most of the current, more serious craze about angels. She contends angels are computer-like in their dependability and somewhat feisty. They are the emissaries from God, capable of monumental feats. But Ms. Baker says

their everyday working guise is more like Tinkerbell instead
of Gabriel or Michael. In fact, she makes a distinction
between our little magical pals and archangels. She has the
only in-depth, first-hand knowledge I know of as to how to
work directly with them, get results and begin to "know"
that they are there for you.

Her life's mission has been to bring joy and self-worth
back to the individual through this Angelic connection,
which she considers everyone's birthright. Now that angels
are finally the "craze," perhaps her mission can finally be
realized. Perhaps the bringing back of joy is the only issue
during this time of high confusion and seriousness. I think
that maybe the only terminal illness is seriousness itself. We
have taken life too seriously and seem to be coming out of
a dark time of a belief system based upon survival and misunderstanding. Perhaps deity is not an angry God and the
Earth is not a penal colony.

There have been more than 100 new books written on
angels in the last few years. They finally made the cover of
Time magazine with the caption, "Everybody believes in
angels, what in heaven is going on?" From this source a
world survey reveals that over 68 percent of adults and 75
percent of teenagers now believe in the existence of angels.
There may be hope for the human race after all.

Another aspect of Ms. Baker's channeled work is quite
controversial and shines a new light on biblical scripture.
The main thrust deals with the Ten Commandments and the
absence of joy, both in the Bible and on the Earth. This
approach, along with what has been discovered in the Dead
Sea Scrolls (that is being stifled and kept from the public)
will split organized religion down the middle, causing a religious revolution. This exposure of certain scripture in light
of modern psychology will lift a dark veil from our approach
to deity. The premise, as with all Hawaiian wisdom, is

simple. Has orthodoxy worshipped two Gods? The one of anger who would have his children born in sin and misery, and the parent of joy that all good parents would choose to emulate. Ms. Baker's interpretations challenges the very *kapu* (forbidden) system of rules that underlies the thinking of our world. It is my prediction that her work, and I hope a few contributions on my part in this area, will be a "shout," sooner or later heard around the world. This is only part of what may be heard from the gathering of voices in the special place that the world knows as Paradise.

Our first collaboration revealed that Ms. Baker's training with the Essene is in direct alignment with the ancient Hawaiian approach to deity. Because of Miriam's 50 years of hands-on experience with angelology, my former associate Patti Anspach and I have been able to see a bridge in the gap of the ancient Hawaiian wisdom. I had already been in the process of trying to prove that the Hawaiian wisdom of *huna* is the same wisdom as other tribal peoples around the world. With Ms. Baker's input, it now appears that the ancients also had a very real working connection with the angels!

It was Patti who discovered perfect Hawaiian descriptions of "secret invisible energies" clearly identifying the angelic realm. Various interpretations of the Hawaiian words associated with angels clearly describe the qualities associated with Ms. Baker's work as distinguished from the popular craze about angels. There is no mention of the large winged creatures of biblical scripture in her teachings, other than they can make themselves appear so if we need the assurance. She says that they are more sprite-like and are made of pure energy, being electrical in nature. Hawaiian descriptions identify them as "small flying persons" made of the same source as our breath of life. The sacred holy light that flies, jump, darts and leaps back and forth from the invisible to the finite bringing brightness, clarity and connection.

Ms. Baker says that two are assigned us from birth on the playground, Earth, to protect us and fetch us our needs.

Ms. Baker's approach may be the missing link to bridging this invisible realm, a connection that has eluded mankind—and many women—since our metaphorical "fall from grace." Like the Hawaiian teaching, her guidelines are simple. If we will but consider our invisible friends and talk with them as we did when we had our innocence, this simple notion will lift us out of the scary world that tempts us to scheme our way through life. Just the notion that you have extra help is a joyful one. Give it a shot and join the miracle workers.

Heiau of the Mermaid

"A million years ago the world split in two. I think I was five or six when it happened. I awoke stranded, alone, with a lump in my throat. I have spent my life trying to find my friends again. My fading memory of their real world has made me grow old."

—From the diary of Wendy,
the winter years and thoughts of Peter.

On the road to *Ho'okena,* the last of a few little beaches on your way south to volcano, there is another special little *heiau* known only to a few Hawaiians. It is another place of feminine, mystical energy on private land and in the stewardship of women only, until recently. Through the bushes by four-wheel drive will bring you out on the blustery, rugged coast setting from another time. I had the honor of being the first man to have stewardship of this *heiau* in over 30 years and its wonderful little coffee shack on the beach. There exists nothing but raw nature and a few seclusive private residences dotting the coastline. The experience comes complete, with no electricity or phone. It is here where I felt like Ernest Hemingway and James Michener for three wonderful months of healing. The *heiau* itself is a magical piece of real estate, predominant as a bright green oasis among the other dead wood, sandy areas. On the property, less than 100 meters from shore, is a brackish pond with a grassy knoll in the middle. At one side is a painted tree stump, acknowledging the sacred energy, where local Hawaiians still leave their offerings.

One incredible starry night when I was feeling the loneliness of my former marriage and its unrealized dreams, the silence was shattered as a wild boar ripped up one of the neighbor's dogs. The dog's face was peeled in half. First aid stitches and a pursuing hunt by the locals filled the remainder of the evening. The brutality of it all triggered my emotions and Vietnam flashbacks of the sounds of gunfire in the jungle. By 11 P.M. I had almost come apart myself. In an effort pagan to my Christian upbringing, I found myself making a flower offering and praying at the little *heiau*.

After some time in silence, around midnight a most unusual thing happened. While I was looking at the full moon a sound came from behind me. This time a gentle one out of a soundless night. It was crystalline, like a delicate windchime, except since the onslaught of hogs and dogs there hadn't been a breeze. I turned toward the grassy knoll in the middle of the pond to witness a startling little revelation. Just above the knoll there was forming a gold iridescent glow. Slowly it grew into a spherical shape. And then, within the translucent, glowing sphere appeared a beautiful, miniature girl.

I know what you are thinking. What was on the label of the dinner I drank that night? Well, I had been chemical-free for some time and that's not the end of the story. Yes, it is true that I had come to Hawaii to connect with the real magic in life, supported by a belief system ready for anything. But this was beyond my expectation. I couldn't see any fins but I knew she must be a mermaid. She appeared as only about three feet in height and when she slipped into the water there was a definite splash and that chime sound again. I blinked and shook my head several times, surmising that I had just had a good hallucination. I would have left it at that and still been thankful for the experience, but then she appeared again. First a glow under the brambles, then her little head above the water, with a wry smile that seemed to say, "That's right. I'm real. Now plug this one into your old worn-out reality."

I felt humbled and must have bowed Japanese fashion for days afterward—but there is more.

My mother and two sisters had the rare treat of joining me there. It was a few days that they will never forget, particularly my Mom, the elf in our family who also had the same experience, describing the encounter perfectly.

When the owner of the property returned some months later I told her of the experience in detail. The absolute dumbfounded look on her face was all the proof I will ever need to know that my experience was not just my conjecture and the empathy of a beloved parent. Ester had been sworn to secrecy by a Hawaiian *kahuna* when she purchased the land to never reveal the details of the *heiau*, unless someone had had a mystical encounter there and was able to describe certain details. She had never taken it seriously through the years, having never had an actual encounter herself. Evidently the old *kahuna* in his 80s and a drunken sailor had been the only ones in this century to witness the mermaid of myth and legend. I had described her as he had, the details in her hair coloring, features and size, and oh yes, the chimes that herald the doorway to the fairy realm.

The owner has sold the property since then, her life path or the spookiness of events taking her elsewhere, I don't know which. The stewardship went to male hands, a soul not appreciative of magic and the like. Word is he has gated the property, forbidding even the locals to leave their blessings. He won't last long on this island.

I will always be grateful for the experience and for another tale for my grandchildren's campfires. For me the magic of Disney's dream had returned to the earthly realm. Since then I have begun to believe again and dream. I have come to the conclusion that everything that has been dreamed about has a physical reality somewhere. In a world half gone mad, this was the night that Peter rediscovered Tinkerbell.

If your world has become seriously ill I suggest that you drop everything, open your heart and look for her once again yourself. The only reason you may not see is from living within the "comfort zone" of an ordinary reality. It has been thousands of years and an old doorway seems to be opening. We had a glimpse before we lost our innocence . . . all of us, invisible playmates from the real world, a world where pain is the illusion. Could it be that there is only one issue in the world that seems to be coming to an end? Maybe it all simply means that it is time to bring the "Joy" back in to our lives.

Waipio: Valley of the Spirits

One of the three must-sees in all the islands is *Waipio,* the Valley of the Kings. My personal other two "musts" are the volcano (when she is birthing) and the *Napali* Coast on the monastery island of *Kaua'i.*

My friends, who are artists and psychics, have stewardship of two charming bed-and-breakfast cottages at the top of the valley. Men will swoon and women will pound their chests when visiting these exhilarating sanctuaries. The view is absolutely breathtaking, one of the most incredible sights in the world. The spectacular *Hi'ilawe* Falls of legend and song, one of the tallest waterfalls in the world, is at the back and far side of Waipio Valley. It is inaccessible lately, which is a darn shame. Many of the residents are hermits who have resigned from the 20th century altogether and there is some dark energy down there, so watch your step. There are also a few wealthy eccentrics living there who value their privacy.

The best way to access the valley for the first time is to take the tram (local land rover or van service) down to the beach and then hoof it on your own and have a picnic. Stupid new rules and some belligerence on the part of locals are making it more difficult for visitors to connect fully with this magnificent wonder of the world. Trail rides and bus tours are now confined to a main road forbidding passage to the beaches and the far side of the valley.

If the river is low and not raging, get wet, ford the stream and walk the beach to the other side of the valley. You will love the outing.

There is a knoll on the other side, with palms that will thrust you into the feeling of an old movie like *South Pacific*. If some idiot littered, just pick up a little, which will be your loving contribution to nature. Then pretend you are the first to ever set foot there.

In the palms and jungle about a third of the way down the beach is a *heiau*. You may "feel it" on your way over. *Do not disturb.*

Waipio has "dark" and "light" energies and a history of drugs, so, as I said, stay away from the residents and remain near the shore or on the main dirt road.

All the tour services are having great difficulty with the residents of Waipio. I can see both sides of the issue, considering myself to be a bit of a rebel and an individualist. But it is a handful of residents trying to keep the world from experiencing one of the truly beautiful destinations.

I would probably be more on the side of the little guy if their efforts were for a shared park or refuge, rather than to keep it just for themselves. This is all fueled by another fire, the larger Hawaiian Sovereignty movement, an issue which needs addressing at the core level.

If the residents would compromise, they could regulate tourism and everything that goes on there while creating a nice income for maintaining roads, trails and the ecology of the entire valley. This is called stewardship, a word that all Hawaiian residents must sooner or later relearn if they are to remain in Paradise. Hawaii is for the world to come and visit during our most defining time in all history.

In the interim, while the feud continues, you can help by listening to your tour guides, staying on the allowed trails and picking up an extra candy wrapper or two.

Another great, safe, first impression of Waipio is the Mule Wagon Tour. The mules like to feel their oats so let the kids sit up front, and don't tell them about the mules' digestive temperament (this is one of our little chuckle initiations).

Your wagon-master Peter, a valley resident, is from England and has been conducting this service for over 15 years. He is one of us who came to get away from it all and is a likable bridge to your vagabond self, as is Sherry, a very spiritual lady who runs the two-hour trail rides.

For your second trip to Waipio you will want to stay for a while, but remember that the valley is only accessible by four-wheel drive and some of the residents can be down-right nasty. We recommend taking an authorized tour. Most tours and rides pass by the little Tomagaki cabins, which are another real find few people know about. Last I heard they were under $20 a night, bring your own linen. There are no phones or electricity so you'll have to book them through the Waipio Shuttle & Four-Wheel Drive Service. Call information on the island and ask for Ann.

A new venture in remote tourism at several hundred dollars a day is "The Tree House." It was dreamed into reality by a retired socialite, a remarkable lady who has retreated into a self-imposed exile away from the humdrum of the modern frenzy. Lovers take great delight in spending a moment in her dream, to be admired by the rest of us who have not had the will or the resources to pursue such a departure from the maddening crowds.

The Tree House cabanas are located deep in the jungle all the way to the rear of the valley, underneath a waterfall. It is like stumbling onto a fairy village straight out of folklore. One of its cabanas is actually built in a huge tree with showers and even a flushing toilet all provided by nature. For the folks who like to rough it with the avant-garde, it is a picture book memory and a get-away-from-it-all Hemingway experience. It still amazes me how the trucks can forage through the impassable jungle and streams to bring you to this other world. The only drawback is mosquitoes, but the owners are very thoughtful in putting effective punks along the lighted trails every evening. The most unforgettable wedding I have ever performed was next to the beautiful waterfall there. Just that memory of connecting with Eden should keep Dion and Andrea married forever.

Now for the fun stuff, the legends. Way on the other side of the valley in the brambles, there is "sometimes" a cave that is said in legend to be the entrance to the underworld. I say "sometimes" because twice I went and it wasn't there. Don't ask for an explanation, I have just learned to accept it as I have other things that defy traditional laws of nature here on the island. A *kahuna* would just yawn and say, "Yeah, it figures."

A fear-based *kapu* legend says that this is a doorway to the underworld and the spirits of little people will drag you in, never to be seen again. This is true of the wet caves in *Kau'ai* where many have been lost in the labyrinths of lava tube caverns.

Although there are thousands of miles of lava tube caves on this island, I have not yet been able to substantiate the same circumstances as *Kau'ai* in this case. Here I have only heard stories that prickle your neck hair and give a definite gut-anxiety feeling when you are in the vicinity of the place.

I did meet one German lady who had intuited the legend and felt the energy when hiking back there. She says that they are "friendly" spirits of the mole people, Earth's inner inhabitants. I would have thought her crackers if I had not had so many far-out experiences here myself and if she had not tracked the legend to that approximate location.

There is also a natural pyramid within the valley (at least it was there the last time I looked). It is one of three known on the island and is swathed in myth.

This one has to do with the cave to the underworld connection. The tale says that only the *kahuna,* sounding a tone through the chant, can open these "doorways" and step into another dimension.

What I found to be curious is the way that this legend came to me from three unrelated sources. Two are respected Hawaiian sources from different family lineages and islands. The third is a Master of the Far East who experienced it in a dream while visiting the island.

The Legend of King's Rock

At the north end of the Big Island, near the sleepy town of *Hawi,* is a large 750-pound rock in the middle of the road. It is about the size and weight of a General Motors V-8 diesel engine block.

It was carried there by King Kamehameha all the way up from the floor of Waipio Valley. He used only his own brute strength. King Kamehameha the Great was over seven feet tall and considered a god among men.

Legend has it that when the Man in White returns to his people, he shall lift that same rock with ease as a symbol that the order of *Kane-Wahine* (balanced male and female understanding) has returned, the High Order of Father/Mother God and balance has come back full circle and returned to reign.

The rock shall be lifted, not by macho brute force, but in the manner of true power beyond power of the legend of the *Menehune*. It will be lifted without effort or force, as a symbol of the deeper understanding of the higher connection. It will be lifted in the name of joy above magic by simply leaving its weight behind.

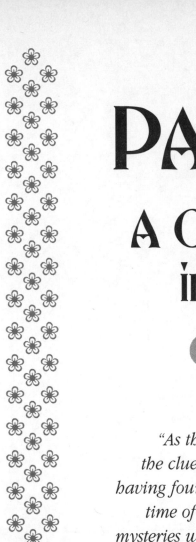

PART III

A Crossroad in Time

*"As they came full circle
the clues were in plain sight,
having found the key within. In the
time of greatest change, the
mysteries were unraveled, revealing
that there was nothing new
under the sun. And the End became
the Beginning, pieces of the
great puzzle finally
fitting together."*

Twelve

A New Look
at Ancient Wisdom

The Cross of Light is a traditional Hawaiian symbol. The four crosses around the outside symbolize the highest energies that represent the four elements: air, fire, water and Earth. The cross in the center holds all the others in place and represents the fifth element, spirit. The optical illusion of the symbol, as well as odd and even numbers, represent the thresholds between higher and lower dimensions of reality.

Huna: The Original Power and Way of Life

Huna is the name encompassing the ancient Hawaiian art and science of psychology and metaphysics. Keeping in mind that a single word can have 50 different meanings depending on the context, I will give you my favorite meaning for Hawaii's ancient wisdom. In recent years *huna* has come to mean "secret" or "knowledge or power withheld from common knowing." *Huna* actually means the invisible essence or life-force. *Huna* is not only a belief system but also a way of life. For Hawaiians and other indigenous peoples it unites the heart and mind. It is about expressing love through acknowledging this great power and recognizing it as the eternal wellspring within ourselves and the foundation stone of the universe.

Hawaiians say that each person comes into this life with a calabash, a bowl of light *(kukui)* that illuminates our path through life, a light that we can share with others. *Huna* teaches the utterly simple ways to connect with this inner bowl of light, which is the substance of our true nature beneath the layers of misconception and the roles we play. It is also the essence of true power connected to the one source of all power. The Hawaiians call this true nature the *Aumakua* or High Self.

Huna consists of universal truths that are accurate, consistent laws of nature and the Universe. A tiny scientific glimpse of these laws has made up the foundation for our contemporary breakthroughs in quantum and atomic physics. The original wisdom has proven powerful enough to have survived through historical events that threatened to eradicate it. These events caused *huna* to be carried underground by a secret order of stewards known as *kahunas*. Literally translated, *huna* means secret. It more clearly means the essence or life-force, that which is invisible to the ordinary, but is the true substance of life.

Connecting with our inner light and experiencing our *Aumakua* allows us to experience the basic unity and order that is the fundamental underlying factor of the Universe. Our *Aumakua,* our true self, allows us to understand our place in the picture or larger tapestry that is all life. Knowing this relationship we can come to share this light of understanding with the world as our unique expression and individual gift.

As a premise of the interconnectedness of the tapestry of life, Hawaiians understand the existence of *mana,* the mysterious invisible force of vital life energy. They believe (as modern science is beginning to prove) that everything including people, gods, rocks, trees, and even words and thoughts carry *mana,* and that this force can be increased and transferred from one source to another. The concept of *mana* surrounds and permeates Hawaiian thought and life, bridging the invisible and the feeling of separateness that we experience while living in a three-dimensional, seemingly finite universe.

Hawaiians are able to increase their *mana* through specific breathing techniques. This is one of the most important and simple elements in their mastery of the life-force. Breath is so important to the Hawaiian *mana* that when the white men came to Hawaii they were called *haole,* a sad term meaning "without the breath of life." Specifically, the white men were called "breathless" because the Hawaiians observed that the missionaries didn't practice breathing techniques before they prayed. (This probably occurred after they were told to close their eyes and pray Christian-style, then opened their eyes to discover that all their land had been taken.)

Hawaiians clearly understood, thousands of years before modern psychology and physiology, how we are structured, the greater wisdom of which still eludes the scientific mind. They knew that, beyond Freud and similar to Carl Jung's model of the human psyche, the best way to understand our function was to consider ourselves in three aspects of one wholeness.

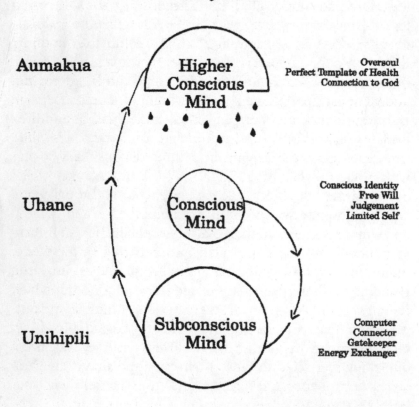

The Trinity of YOU

Aumakua — Higher Conscious Mind — Oversoul / Perfect Template of Health / Connection to God

Uhane — Conscious Mind — Conscious Identity / Free Will / Judgement / Limited Self

Unihipili — Subconscious Mind — Computer / Connector / Gatekeeper / Energy Exchanger

©1992 Pila, Psychological Trends of Hawaii

The conscious, rational mind which directs our decisions and controls our will power is called the *unhane.* This is the thinking self, sometimes in Hawaiian wisdom known as the lazy or forgetful self. This is what we come to know as our identity but the Hawaiians know is really the smallest part and we are much, much more than that! The unconscious mind, the seat of emotions, memories and habits is called the *unihipili,* the feeling self. This is a greater part of us, like an enormous computer reserve, that runs the body, files all memory and experience, has a connection to the higher realms and co-creates our heartbeat. The superconscious, the higher mind and the connection to the source of light and higher realms is the *Aumakua* or "spiritual over-soul." I depict this aspect of self as a protective, encompassing umbrella.

The three selves are actually one unit; therefore, created to live in harmony, each is doing its part to maintain balance and the optimum functioning of the individual. The unconscious was not considered an uncontrollable beast (as in the earlier concepts of modern psychology) but a very loving and powerful child (as reflected in the current "inner child" movement in psychology) . . . a child who functions literally and quite simply, much like a computer.

Hawaiians clearly understood the relationship and interdependence of the three selves to an extent beyond anything that has been observed in our modern sciences of the mind to a point of being able to perform great magic as well as miracles of healing. Hawaiians believed that total wellbeing could be maintained through the integration of heart and mind and expressed it as a holistic way of life. They believed that the *Aumakua,* High Self, held a template of perfect, youthful health which is our natural state and anything less than that was to be considered a simple misunderstanding that could be rectified.

They knew that the path to the light of the High Self is

through the unconscious, and that the clearing of blocks of negative emotions, guilt, fixations and complexes in the unconscious allows a function and communication at this level. They contended that the High Self is an utterly trustworthy spirit self who is there to guide and help us when we ask—but we have to ask. When this connection to High Self is open it is said that the blessings of Heaven rain down upon one like a fragrant, purple mist. The evidence of this connection being so is whenever we experience joy or bliss in our lives. This is considered to be a force more powerful than any event, obstacle or circumstance. This force comes from within, opening the floodgates of the connection. The direction of the uninterrupted flow from High Self is achieved by this mystical, elusive angle called *kulana*. *Kulana* means attitude. When the angle is correct (a slant) and the attitude is one of joy within and an appreciation for life, nothing in the ordinary world can prevail over that "force from Heaven."

Note your greatest experiences in life and check out this angle. How about the rich and famous? What is their slant? Could it all be this simple? Simplicity is the Hawaiian key to all wisdom. Consider for a moment how powerful you would be if you felt good and had an attitude of joy no matter what was going on around you. Would you be the one that shines the light in a crowd? Could that be the clue to charisma and magnetism . . . even the attraction of wealth and fame? The ancient Hawaiians say that unlimited power with the force of a flood (and yet as gentle as a soothing mist) can be released through this angle of a connection.

The ancient Hawaiians knew of practical ways to communicate with the High Self, maintain that *kulana* (which also means high station or prominent rank) to live in harmony through the practice of the following concepts:

- The *ohana* (family attitude) was the center of life, and there were continual *ho'oponopono* (setting relationships right) sessions to ensure against misunderstandings and the harboring of ill will.
- *Kala* (to release) was the technique for mental and emotional cleansing of negative emotions, particularly sin and guilt, in order to maintain one's life path clearly. (That slant, attitude for releasing the floodgates, is also called *Kala-na,* which also means to filter or examine.)
- *Mihi* (repentance) was the asking and giving of forgiveness, to purge that which is unnecessary to hold on to and thereby "flow in harmony" again.
- *Lokahi* (agreement) was the practice of unity with the great spirit, to maintain peace by adjusting to the proper alignment.
- *Malama* (to take care of) was the service to Humankind and nature, to tend to—stewardship.
- Throughout all Hawaiian thought and life is the concept of *aloha. Aloha* is love. It is light. It is spirit. It is living from our hearts. *Alo* means to "stand in the presence of" or "to go with." *Ha* is the breath, the essence of spirit and light, that connection which the life force rides upon. To say *"ALOHA"* is to stand in the presence of the breath, spirit and light and to acknowledge and recognize all of this in another.

This was once the simple formula for keeping the attitude that prevailed for all. There was no sickness that could not be healed. There was no act that could not be forgiven and sorted out. It was Paradise, but even when the Garden was in complete harmony there were times of confusion, because that is the nature of the earthly realm. Whenever the lessons of life dealt a blow—whenever there was a hurt it was said that this could sometimes add a rock to your

bowl of light and yes, sometimes, even in paradise, your
entire calabash of light could be blocked out by being filled
with rocks from the sometimes harsh lessons of life. But the
Children of the Rainbow knew something else that modern
society has forgotten. No matter what the pain and confusion life may have dealt us—no matter how many rocks get
into our bowl, there is a way to heal all and get our bowl
of light *(kukui)* back. These were the ways to turn the bowl
over and dump the rocks. And dumping the rocks was all
there was to it.

Kahunas: The Great
Sorcerers And Magicians

Kahuna: Steward of the Secret Force, Master of the
Invisible Essence.

The *kahunas* of old Hawaii were the keepers of the
secrets and experts in any one of many particular fields. A
priestly or spiritual *kahuna* was simply a person whose
mind was preoccupied with the larger picture, or thoughts
of God and therefore achieved calm and dignity of spirit.

In ancient Hawaii, the *kahuna* carefully shared these
secrets in exclusive teachings and initiations. They were
considered as trusted by the gods to keep the secrets of
nature protected, while using the wisdom to help mankind.

Then there came a time in more recent history, called the
time of *kapu,* when this knowledge was withheld. In this
new age we may begin to see through the power struggle
and discover that the truth can be revealed to all those who
take the time to study and explore its revelations.

Any true master of a trade could be considered a *kahuna,* but the true understanding of the title extended beyond
the trade into a wisdom that encompassed universal principles

applying to all life. There were many specialty skills of the *kahuna* that encompassed powers such as creating weather, shape-shifting, teleportation and even directing the flow of lava from the volcano. With the help of the Hawaiian shaman teaching of Dr. Serge King, some of those skills can be identified as:

Ho'o maika'i: The skill of blessing.
Piko-piko: The skill of energizing power centers.
Ike Papalua: The skill of shifting to another level of awareness.
Noho: The skill of channeling.
Ka'ao: The skill of storytelling.
Kahi: The skill of healing with dual focus.
Ho'omanamana: The skill of empowerment.
Kaulike: The skill of balancing/integrating the body.
Hailona: The skill of tuning into the past, present and future.
La'a Kea: The skill of energizing and healing aka fields.
Haipule: The skill of manifesting events and circumstances.
Kulike: The skill of shape-shifting.
Mo'ike: The skill of interpreting dreams.
Makaku: The skill of creative dreaming.
Komo Po: The skill of shaman journeying.
Kimana: The skill of increasing personal energy.
Nalu: The skill of contemplative manifestation.
Kalana hula: The skill of focused movement.
Ho'ailona: The skill of healing with symbols and omens.
Hana La'a: The skill of ritual and ceremony.
Kuhikuhipu'u'one: The skill of geomancy.
Hele Kikilo: The skill of time travel.
Kahoaka: The skill of magical flight.
Kukulu Kumuhana: The skill of working with group energy.

The real meaning of the title *kahuna* acknowledges a mastery which embraces universal principles beyond the mechanics of any given trade. This produced a sage gifted with "seer" ability pertaining to all life. They applied their skill to any field of specialization which pertained to their aptitude or interest. Some liked to doctor, some liked to surf. Others liked to travel interdimensionally.

Here we are interested in the ancient Hawaiian alchemists. This is the controversial door that has been closed for centuries due to fear and the abuse of power. The final thread of connection was all but skillfully severed by the Caucasian onslaught, outlawing its practice. Few today realize that even the pronunciation of the language was altered to destroy the resonance of certain words in a further effort to render the *kahuna* powerless.

Laws were instilled making it illegal for any two Hawaiians known as *kahunas* to socialize in public. The remainder of these laws was only recently removed from the statutes in the last few years. This all happened to the Hawaiian people because ancestral guilt played a role in the acceptance of their downfall and the destruction of their own powers. It could have had to do with human sacrifice. The *kahunas* had abused their mastery and this soul memory was passed on unconsciously to be absolved in the future. All peoples, with the exception of a few isolated island cultures, have passed through the same fate. It was too late, after first observing the newly arrived white priests in ritual, that they realized the missionaries did not have the power of their own *kahunas*. The Hawaiians attributed this lack of power in the white priests to their simple failure to make the correct higher connection by breathing properly before they prayed. To this day foreigners are called by the same name they gave these powerless priests. They were called *haole,* which means "without the connection to the breath of life."

Before *kapu* (anything forbidden), when the reverent connection with all life was greatest, so was the power of the *kahuna*. Understanding their nuclear and quantum physical interrelatedness with nature, the *kahunas* were the greatest of sorcerers and magicians. With the simple use of breath to elevate the body's vibration, tone to alter its energy field and the mind power of visualization to materialize the altered form, the *kahuna* could polarize his entire neurology, attracting and projecting lightning itself from the clouds. A *kahuna* would become the lightning rod, drawing the energy of the clouds to his back through the excitement of the life force coiled at the base of the spine and loins. The force was then pulled up, rippled over the shoulders and projected with the hands, again with the breath and tone. To this day, on the Big Island, it is said that these "fireballs" can be witnessed at night.

This phenomenon has been witnessed in nature during mid-western electrical storms. In Joplin, Missouri, when I was growing up, an occasional "soccer ball" of electrical energy would travel down the street in a leisurely fashion, scaring the hell out of all who witnessed it. A remnant of the ability to artificially produce this phenomenon is found in the Filipino ability to kindle paper into flame. A lack of mastery in this area is the bizarre phenomenon of spontaneous human combustion, where the energy field becomes unfocused and polluted in thoughts of denial which have screwed up the chemistry of the body to a point of "melt down."

As with teleporting ("beaming down") on the series "Star Trek" and sound blasting in the movie *Dune,* further clues to the masteries of energy that the *kahunas* once knew are riddled throughout our own science-fiction folklore.

Similar mastery to the *kahuna* skills can be found in other tribal cultures. Ancient chants I have recently decoded insinuate that these legendary powers were present in the Hawaiian culture until recently. Their remnants remain intact in present-day Hawaii more forcefully than anywhere else in the world because of the isolation of the islands and the climate. Hawaii is the most geographically remote place on Earth where the need to survive against nature did not suppress the wisdom through male domination, as has predominantly happened elsewhere. This has to do with the male will suppressing female intuition, which is the aspect of our psyche that is the ability to connect to the higher realms. It is evident in the older chants and folklore that until the *kapu* System was instilled, women were in equal power to men as *kahunas*.

The Hawaiian Chant: Coded Secrets to the Mysteries

"In the beginning was the sound . . . and the sound was with God and the sound was God. Recent translations suggest that this is every bit as valid a translation of the Bible as the more widely known "In the beginning there was the word . . ."

In the new world of quantum physics we have come to learn that all structure contains its own tone much like a chord played on a piano. This cord binds the atoms together into molecules, with groups of molecules forming the matter we can see with the naked eye, such as a chair, a rock or the human form. Ancient Hawaiian wisdom embraced this knowledge thoroughly, possibly thousands of years before our current knowledge of the nature of the atom. It appears that at one time through the applied wisdom of *huna,* the *kahuna* could *play* the notes that vibrated with the individual and even *rearrange* them. They could strike a *tone* at will and rearrange the human body so that anything less than youthful perfection was rearranged and put back in order.

The early Hawaiians more fully understood the human body, not as a dense pile of flesh, but for the quantum mechanical energy-field that it really is. They also understood a deeper interaction with the environment and contended that the body could be *transported* as well as *transformed.* It is all in the records more concise than written documents, known as the Hawaiian Chant.

The chant, with its musical inflection and accompanying *hula,* define and contextualize meaning more accurately than the written word. Symbols dashed off on paper are easily misunderstood, as evidenced by all the holy wars fought over the same scriptures.

This is because all meaning is context-dependent and paper never gives the full context, in fact quite the opposite. A simple inflection in how a word is pronounced may give it an entirely different meaning.

One should never take a book or novel literally, for it is *such stuff as dreams are made of.* An effectively written book is at best a trigger for the imagination that can effectively cause us to paint our own pictures. This could explain the squabbling that has been responsible for so much bloodshed in the name of sacred scripture throughout history.

The chant expressed through the *hula* further supports and preserves the meaning of the words by the use of the body in the pantomiming and acting out of the message. When I was first intuitively led to decoding the chant in the early 1970s I found more than one level of profound metaphysical (beyond the physical) meaning hidden in them.

A look at a simple, popular entry chant for the *hula* will demonstrate this point. Today, even most Hawaiians think that this chant just means "we are coming through the door and starting to dance." But the Hawaiian language always has a deeper meaning for those who choose to listen. For someone familiar with the ancient Egyptian wisdom that speaks of certain stars, such as Sirius, as being "doorways" and the notion of the Big Island of Hawaii as also being a "doorway" of some kind, then the meaning of this simple chant takes on astounding implications:

> Ho'o puka e ka la
> Ma ka hi kinae
> Me kahua ka'i hele no tumutahi
> Ha'a mai nai, iwa me hiiaka
> Me tapo Laka ika ulu wehiwehi
> Ne'e mai nai, iwa ma ku'u alo
> Ho'i no'o e te tapu, me na' Ali'i e
> E ola makou, a mau loa lae
> Ea la, ea la, ea
> A ie, ilei, ie, ie, ie

Decoded:

Open the aperture (doorway) to the sun itself and reveal the source, the light behind the (illusion) of the (blinding) light. Like the sunrise of a new day, dawn upon me, (metaphorically) enlighten me. From the foundation (source) lift up; move from the unknowable (unfathomable) origin. Through the breath (at the angle) come to me, take me by force loudly, lap me up, cradle me, oh light. Spinning, take me, drift upon me, increase, spread, decorate me as this song, change me, purge me, conduct through me the God-force of life. Drape over, course through, purge my being. By my surrender, come and be with me. Cause to come to me (re-member) the sacred most high, intense clarity of being. Sustain me, nurture forever (within me) this permanent mental quality of wisdom.

He inoa no, ma ka Hikina

The honored song that brings in the dawning of enlightenment.

The Hawaiian chant further contains several specific levels of meaning, here to instruct the body to rearrange itself to receive this enlightenment at the cellular level. Other levels of meaning in the chant have to do with connecting and communing with the immediate environment as well as having an affect upon it.

The first time I fiddled with these "tones" and began to fathom their intent I was on the fly bridge of my boat in the middle of a lightning storm in Catalina Island. What ensued was a "coincidental" cooperation of the elements where the lightning across the horizon then marched toward me. I have never had such a thrilling or terrifying experience since Vietnam and was very glad that it stopped cooperating within a mile of the boat. Since that experience while chanting, I have had dozens of witnesses at similar "coincidental" events of clouds and rain and other energy phenomena. My little buddy, Jennifer Anspach, could bring the sun out on any rainy day, anytime she performed the *Ho'opuka* chant. The Hawaiians called her an Old Soul of Hawaiian Wisdom at age 11.

Through the years, others have crossed my path who are working with "tonal" research. A gentleman from Texas at one of our international seminars formed mandalas and other art using beautiful musical vibrations to affect sand (crystal silica). Now computers can mathematically interpret tone, bringing beautiful patterns to music where we can begin to visualize some of what the ancient *kahunas* were connecting with. Another Big Island resident, Tony Selvage, is a remarkable "New Age" musician whom many believe to be the reincarnation of Chopin. He has been featured on dozens of recordings playing his electric viola. Tony has the ability to compose your "akashic song," the music of you. The most important note here is that it is a matter of scientific record that Tony has killed cancer cells with his incredible "music (tone) of the soul."

Another way of beginning to fathom the *kahuna's* understanding and practice of changing matter, is that the chant seems to "sound the tone" that can rearrange and unlock neurology to receive certain "higher signals." My studies are now directed towards certain chants to see if "cosmic records" in human DNA can be retrieved and accessed through tone. The meaning and actual sounds of Hawaiian words can attract and repel energy. Their meanings also have to do with capturing, molding and transforming energies.

I have had an unusual response coast to coast to my live Hawaiian meditation journeys. People are seeing the same images and having deep, emotional responses, as if we had all been around some sort of ancient campfire together, long, long ago. Could sound be the skeleton key that unlocks the vast library of our DNA? Another enigma has been an unexplainable, deep emotional response to the Hawaiian chant in my seminars across the country and in Europe. I find it particularly interesting with people who have never had any connection with Hawaii whatsoever . . . at least in this lifetime.

If you do not have access to a recording of the ancient Hawaiian sound, try evoking it yourself and see what happens with the feelings in your neurology and the pictures in your mind. Here is the simple pronunciation for the vowels:

A is pronounced ah	U is pronounced as in you, ooo
E " " eh	W is pronounced va
I " " eee	Au is ow, as in ouch
O " " oh	Ai is pronounced eye

You will know when you do perform the chant correctly because the words will "ring true" and give you a buzz. Everyone who can should take a couple of voice lessons, at least until you find what is known in voice study as your fundamental tone. Any good voice teacher can help you. When you speak or sing in your "fundamental tone," it "rides in the breath" and will resonate your whole body. Without effort an opera student can shake the windows in a four-story building. Go back to the section on the volcano and ritual to Madame Pele and try the prosperity chant "E Laka E" first. Hundreds of students have told me that singing this simple chant during the day, whenever they are alone, driving or just happen to think of it, quickly elevates their *kaulana* (attitude) giving them a better "slant" on things. It is said to be the sound that opens the floodgates to generating prosperity.

Let us take a look at some other Hawaiian chants. The following is the chant used to open the International Merrie Monarch Hula Festival in Hilo, Hawaii on the Big Island.

> *Ku mai ka puulena*
> *Mai ka uka mai o Kilauea*
> *Popohe lehua popohe ika ua*
> *Ha'a ka ma'um'u i ka noe uka*
> *Ha'a ka lala o ka iliahi*
> *Ahui e hoala ahui ho'ope*
> *Aloha e aloha e*

The ordinary translation given speaks only of the literal, superficial level having to do with environment and location:

> The Puulena wind rises
> from the uplands of Kilauea
> Round is the lehua—rounded in the rain

Bent is the grass of the misty uplands
Bent are the branches of the iliahi
Uniting in fragrance
Aloha e Aloha e

Knowing now what you do about deeper connections and computer access to the unconscious and Higher conscious, can you begin to suspect what is really going on?

The *Pu'ulena* wind is a mysterious cold wind of legend. An element connected with the volcano, Kilauea, that is peaceful and blows towards the village of Hilo on the Big Island. It is always spoken of in sweet sadness, as in the loss of a connection to a precious memory. And speaking of connection, remember the fishing *heiau* where the *kahunas* sounded the round tone like the clanger of a bell that was connected to the bowl of the fish sonar and the bowl of a net? It is said that picking the sacred *lehua* blossoms in Hawaii will bring the tears of Pele, the misty rain. Note the special angles mentioned and the unification achieved in making (ho) fragrance (ala). Ala also means "the path" and "to waken."

The next chant, *Moeuhane,* is more than a chant that just speaks of the ancestors, but may well tell us how to prepare ourselves to experience the different reality of the dream realm:

Moeuhane
(To recall the Spirit into the Dreamtime)

He kanaka loa
He kanaka poko
He ui a'a he, alaneo
A na maka
Pa'i ka lani

Malu ka honua
Ia kama uhili e
He'e ne Ku
I ka Moe au
A ke kahuna

Decoded:

I prepare my being to receive Heaven's energy to stay with me for a long time.

Cradling the spirit energy to quicken me and find grounding within my excited body (awakened neurology).

From the other side, activate the (purple) doorway (the third eye) to open to the still place of burning.

Pass through the open eye swiftly to the Heavens (by the breath like the eye of a needle).

Now allowing all that is withheld (Sacred still remaining) to fling through suddenly.

As I proclaim my child-right again, braid on, intensify in identity.

Spread out, slide-slip (now) melt my rigid structure (body-field and constructs) here, anchoring.

Proclaiming now the Dream as mine (catching the wave, the current as the cycle comes around).

Molded (now) into my reality and ordained absolutely (now) with me as the Master Keeper.

The very thought or sound of the ancient words of the chant can soften the glue on our dense reality. Students who have studied for a short time in Hawaii have told me from around the world of incredible events occurring in their lives connected with the simple use of the chant. The sound delights the body into gooseflesh, gladdens the heart and can alter (elevate) the energy of what is going on around you. One woman relayed her story of a six-car head-on collision in the rain on the L.A. Freeway. A Safeway Food Stores double tractor-trailer had jackknifed in front of her while trying to avoid another car. Instead of being the seventh element of disaster she reports the following:

> *"In the split seconds of the accident I felt a tidal wave of overwhelming fear which caused me to grab my breath. And, then, in the middle of that deep breath, I found myself in a total calm. I guess it was triggered by all the times I had practiced the* Huna *breathing technique. Out came the chant I had learned from you as a jingle and what happened after that was truly marvelous. As my car spun around, it was as if everything were in slow motion and I was outside of myself, at an angle above and to the side. I viewed myself smiling and singing and holding on to the steering wheel in absolute calm. The car must have spun around at least three times, weaving its way through the colliding cars. It righted itself as I continued on to work that day while everyone else involved had a wreck."*
> —Susan M., Santa Monica, California

You don't have to know the meaning of the words for the chant to have an immediate soothing affect upon you. The sounds are pure and the meaning is so abstract that it seems to effect a fundamental change in the substance of the neurology. It's like that beautiful song that moves you emotionally, stirring your soul with a call from forever, even though you may be hearing it for the first time.

Another lady shared with us her startling story of being in a bank hold-up while waiting in the teller line. She said that the perpetrator who waved the gun was a derelict strung out on drugs and that the fear immediately invoked in the crowd was a black cloud that could have been cut with a knife:

> *"I found myself closing my eyes to all of it and humming the words to No hoana (a chant to High Self). I am not good at making pictures in my head but this one was crystal clear. It was as if a tornado of white light poured in on me from above and like, you know the clouds that melting dry ice makes, like they use in theatre productions? Well, it poured in all over the floor around me. So I kept on humming and focusing on the words of the chant and let the clouds of light spread out all around me until it filled the whole bank. I felt this peace and it was as if all the audio of all the confusion around me was turned down . . . and then the funniest thing happened. The guy, the bank robber . . . started crying and turned his gun over to the teller. He was cuffed and whisked off in no time and it was all over. I not only feel like I was able to change my attitude and bring in light to the situation, I feel like I had something to do with it all playing out differently!"*
> —Bonnie C., Los Angeles, California

I have had other reports from as far away as France and South Africa on the power that comes from simply thinking about this next chant to the High Self. It is my favorite and a source of profound insight in my life. To sing it properly as an *oli* (chant not danced to, sung with a trill at the end of each phrase) is to shake the Earth and elevate the body into a sense of good feeling and natural protection. Here is that chant with one of the seven decoded levels of its ominous meaning:

Ai Noho ana Ke Akua
(GOD-LINK: To fathom, reside in and conduct to full
capacity the God-force.)
Ke aloha ai no ho ana ke akua i ka na hele hele
I alai i'a e teti ohu ohu e ka ua koko
E na kino malu i ta lani
Malu e hoe
E ho'o ulu mai, ana o Laka i kona kahu 'owau 'owau noa
Ua i kea

Decoded:
Sound the gong of love, the life-force connection. Come
together, make love to me oh God, conduct through me, put
me in order, until I fathom intensely the divine supernatural
spirit (of light). At the same time, compound, multiply
beyond compare, hurl towards me, divide, fill the grooves of
the frequency, move towards me, unknowable force of God.

Simultaneously capture my eyes (as beauty does) sift,
screen, move as a steady gentle breeze, intensify strangely,
crowd, push, now shoot, blow, form into mist, bringing to
me the fragrance of your essence. Swell like a wave (now)
I become the essence and toss and fling myself upward.
Come to me, rain down upon me (I see now the essence
forming in the mist), rainbow sparkling rain, pregnant with
manifesting energy like seed pods popping . . .

It already is, the peculiar calm feeling, I fly now, I am the
power to fly, the secret safe (feeling enlightening, lighting
my being) simultaneous intensity (elevating my being) to
the heavenly, spiritual, exhalted royalty.

As beforehand the unusual, give me through the hard
breath (the wheezing) make me to receive spirit, be like
godself, entertain within me, inspire me (now) towards me,
come, be welcome within my seat of being, know me (as
sexual surrender without restraint) have your way with me

(oh light of God) full measure, satiate me, satisfy my (longing) fill, I absorb like a sponge, I fill up like a cavernous grotto, encompassing, surrounding (your love).

Chime now, ring true, ring on, undulating, continuing with me forever, existing calm and tamed within my being, lock on like a magnet, I surrender to the God-force, blow through me like the strong leeward wind, I tend in stewardship the current, the flow, now constantly burning intensely, I release all restriction, now surrender into a raging unquenchable fire. Rain over me, rain on me like a storm, I am the same as the storm, the fire. I am now clear, the white pure perfect virile, potent essence of light.

If I had two wishes I think one would be to see that everyone on Earth hear and feel the sound of, and intent behind, this one chant. The second wish would be for everyone to individually come and stand on a Hawaiian high cliff or mountain top to connect with their destiny and remember that chant. I have always been accused of being oversimplistic but I believe to fully understand these notions may be all that is required to take Humankind to the next level of knowing what we are all about. It has been thousands of years since Humankind has even had a glimpse of what we are made of and who we were formed in the image and likeness of. Despite a lousy track record, within us is the stuff of great beauty and passion, animated by the force of all creation.

Hula: A Discipline Beyond the Martial Arts

Do you still think that Hawaiians are just folks who enjoy a good song and dance? Well, even the *hula* has some surprises for you. It has a power beyond the martial arts. The lower, basic forms of the martial arts such as karate oppose energy, battling it head-on in an effort to control it. Higher forms, even Jujitsu, seek to redirect energy by bypassing it or turning it back on itself in an effort to gain control.

The *hula,* however, goes a step further. The dancer seeks initially neither to control nor direct energy. The *hula* teaches that when the energy of the life-force flows uninterrupted from the feet up through the hips (another key) and with joy out through the fingertips, the dancer is in a perfect state of grace with all life.

This is the cooperation that the palm tree shows in her sublime, inseparable dance with the breeze. The dance produces (or reclaims) a sacred ground, a state where no ill will exists, where the dancer is immune to any negative energy—a target for nothing.

The dancer becomes the eye of the storm, a vortex of energy, lost in the song. This is a protection beyond defense, glimpsed only in what can sometimes be characterized as the innocence of a child.

My tribe, the Cherokee, told of Geronimo, Crazy Horse and other great shamans as being in this state of bliss with Great Spirit (without arrogance or defiance) when they demonstrated to their warriors that they would not be hit, even with Gattling guns. They would ride back and forth before their enemies, hands in the air proving that they were the "sacred ground" which attracts only the "joy of being."

Those few who have totally devoted their lives to any martial art beyond black belt to red belt find themselves skipping several levels of spiritual development. Many achieve this level of mastery, finally realizing that there is a "ground" where no fighting exists.

Along with the chant, the hula performs a second function as I have previously mentioned, providing deeper connections and more accurate records of ideas, principles and information beyond the written word. The performance not only relayed the information but also activated neurological connections in the body to subconsciously release information to the conscious mind, a motorized form of triggering psychic response. The physical movements along with the chant also allow the dancer's energy field to interact with the environment on more than one level simultaneously.

My intuitive work in this area is a drop in a new bucket of a different approach to unlocking the secrets of mysticism that have eluded us for centuries. This form of movement coupled with the sounds of the chants give a different perspective to understanding and connecting with energy and vibration.

I compare the new dimensions in this study like progressing from black-and-white film to 3-D, Technicolor, sensurround, with an olfactory option. It is sort of a newly rediscovered foundation stone in the next phase of Virtual Reality "God stuff." Since opening "Pandora's Box" in this new look at ancient wisdom, one of the conclusions I have come to is that the ancient Hawaiians didn't talk about life in a sterile classroom setting. They knew how to take the Disney "E" ticket ride.

Hawaiian Healing

Hawaiian *huna* contends that there is a blueprint for perfect health within the individual and anything can be rectified or healed. The best way to explain the Hawaiian viewpoint is a European interview with a student-friend I met in Hawaii from Germany. On my first world tour in 1994 I was amazed at the reception in Europe towards the Ancient Hawaiian wisdom. Here is the New York interview that predicated the European tour:

"The Interview:"
George Kirkoven—Amsterdam

I am here with author, lecturer and psychic, Pila of Hawaii. First of all let me tell you a little about our guest. Pila is a decorated Vietnam Veteran. During intense combat he received the gift of "seeing" while having an out-of-body experience that shattered his reality. He returned home hollow, to a world torn apart and a straightjacket with his teeth wired shut. Like the rest of the Vietnam legacy, his country and everything it stood for had betrayed him. The next 20 years became a sojourn to find any spiritual purpose for his experience. His visions plagued the long road to recovery spending most of his adult life in some sort of therapy. The road and his vision brought him home to Hawaii. Today, he is a lecturer, therapist and minister involved in the teaching and research of ancient Hawaiian *huna,* the major piece to his extraordinary puzzle. Please welcome William "Pila" Chiles. (applause) Welcome, Pila.

"Aloha, George." "Aloha."

George: Pila, in your work, are there any central ideas in your healing of people?

Pila: Yes, the *huna* approach to healing is simple and is in a total 180 degree opposition to traditional medicine and the Western civilization approach. *Huna* contends that there is nothing broken which needs to be fixed or even mended. The *huna* philosophy implies a perfect template in and back of all manifestation. A template that can be accessed through the clarification, not healing, of understanding. When this "access" is made, what may appear to happen is a healing . . . sometimes instantaneously.

George: What actually is healing?

Pila: In the *huna* approach the proper understanding of healing is clarification in the third dimensional or effectual realm of what is already perfect in the abstract or causal realm. This elevates us out of the realm of Band-aids into the proper premise of perfection.

George: What is in your opinion of illness? Why do people become sick?

Pila: Illness is a simple misunderstanding, although be it sometimes a terrible one. People become sick because of something they are not embracing in their consciousness. The affliction is always symbolic of what is not being embraced in the causal realm. Science now contends that the cells of the body were designed to be immortal and when properly oxygenated are impervious to disease and infection. Hawaiian philosophy says that it is erroneous thought processes that alter that immunity.

George: What is your specific role in the healing?

Pila: It is the role of the *kahuna* to assist the afflicted person in "sorting out" their consciousness and accepting their own ability to heal. The *kahuna* has not the power to heal but the wisdom to assist others in unleashing their own innate and divine power.

George: Do you see any limitations in healings, with other words: do you see sometimes no chance in healing a person?

Pila: I have been personally dealing with terminally ill people since 1986 and have found approximately 15 percent who were non-responsive. I have attributed this to a deep seated conviction that all seemed to have in common. Succinctly, this had to do with an outlook on life of hopelessness, being "worn out" with the insanity of it all. With terminal cancer I have found a single "death wish," a clear decision of "giving up" some two to three years prior to the onset of the disorder. This is usually accompanied by a significant emotional event which caused them to declare hopelessness and has always traced back to a "mind set" established as a child. There are recent studies in NLP (neuro-linguistic programming) and psychology that are beginning to substantiate this syndrome of the mind/body connection with cancer. The *huna* philosophy treats this emotional dam as a blockage of the life-force known simply as a "knot in one's Joy." If the simple techniques of *huna* are embraced it is easy for the *kahuna* to help one "untie the knot," if they are willing. Otherwise, I have found that I have had to honor this "death wish." More documented research needs to be done in this area by qualified psychologists. Other than these instances I have had remarkable "spontaneous remissions" occurring in some 85 percent of the clients sent to me, including many so-called incurable disorders. Because of the pressures of persecution I no longer work directly one-on-one with those afflicted but choose willingly to teach any professional healers with open minds these ancient psychological techniques. As science is now proving that the cells of the body were designed to be immortal, there is no limit to what can be accomplished in this area.

George: In which methods have you been trained?

Pila: None. My work is intuitive. I was led to the Big Island (Hawaii) from a vision I had in heavy combat in Vietnam. In a search for my own answers I have been assisting others in finding their light since the mid-1980s. It is my opinion that these techniques are further evidence of a resurgence of ancient Hawaiian wisdom.

George: On what levels do you heal? Do you heal on the body level, the spiritual level, the mental level or all three at once?

Pila: The spiritual level, usually through a mental

approach in addressing one's Life Purpose or Destiny. The readings that I do are a gift of "seeing" the *akashic* record which I received in Vietnam. The full power of this gift came into effect in the mid-1980s when I began taking the "hopeless" to a special sacred ground on the Big Island called *Pu'uhonua O' Honaunau,* the Place of Refuge. I have found that when addressing a person's "larger picture" and what they are all about, many times their other issues simply clear up. In the ancient tradition, once something was cleared up spiritually and mentally, it was then worked out of the tissues physically, usually through Hawaiian *lomi lomi* massage with a ritual to rid the energy field.

George: How do you make the diagnosis?

Pila: Find out what isn't working in the client's life. There is usually a pattern that can be seen in all areas, from their relationships and career, sometimes even symbolically depicted down to the problem with the car they drive. The Hawaiian approach is that life can be seen simply and what is true in the macrocosm shows similarity in the microcosm.

George: What are the most important healing methods in Hawaii?

Pila: The ones that work.

George: I know that some Hawaiian healers use symbols during their healing work. What is the importance of the symbols and do you use them?

Pila: No. Pictures can help focus if the essence of what they depict is fathomed. A picture can be worth a thousand words but these things are too complicated for me, as well as much of the ritual we tend to become lost in. I suggest using sound vibration instead. The sound of one word could be worth a thousand pictures.

George: What do you mean with "sound vibration" as opposed to healing with symbols?

Pila: The simplest way to understand would be the difference in a mother showing her child pictures to delight him or singing to him. Sound may include any vibration, pentameter or the silent space produced between pentameters, and the sound our word symbols make when uttered until the intent called "love" is conveyed. This intent can be conveyed to balance, reduce or "shake loose" false buildup or to cause complete transformation. I prefer the latter. Why putt around. In "singing" to people's hearts about their purpose (whether they are terminally ill or at any other threshold) I try to evoke a core-level emotional response (vibration) that breaks through all buildup causing a complete transformation. Many healers find this a bit "sticky" and would rather go for a flat emotional response.

George: Is food important to stay or become healthy?

Pila: It is suggested that most folks should stop and eat something at least once every three days or so. Many New Age vegetarians have become so preoccupied with what goes into their bodies that they have this emaciated "green around the gills" look to them. They have become so sensitive to their environments that they gag at a whiff of cigarette smoke from a block away and can no longer dine at public places. It is suggested that many should begin to examine what goes into their minds since the body, like a shark, can damn near digest an alarm clock and still come back from the dead even after such pagan tortures as chemotherapy and even radiation treatment. It is the thoughtfulness and notions of health while eating that nurture the energyfield (the body), releasing or reenergizing the intrinsic factor in food. It is easier to accept the full intent of this by eating good food. Besides, it tastes better.

George: Could one compare the Hawaiian way of healing with one of the more alternative ways of healing, like homeopathy, Ayurveda, spiritual healing, etc?

Pila: All have their roots in *huna* or what I term "the first teaching." Most have complicated the simple truth of the *huna* origin. As my friend Serge King would say, "If it works, it's *huna*." It has been said that there is one light, one truth and many paths leading to the one.

George: These days one hears so much about manifesting or creating and the impact of our thoughts. Did the Hawaiians have specific ideas about that?

Pila: There was a time when manifesting was instantaneous. Manifesting has been hit or miss these days because we have been missing the computer access code until now. Thank God there has been this buffer, otherwise we would have a very cluttered world filled with the half-baked thoughts of what people think they want. Over the past two decades I have intuited part of this access code to share. My work over the last year with a very special metaphysician and healer, Dr. Paula Culp of St. Paul, Minnesota has us very close to the final key. It should transform prosperity seminars. Thought force is behind all manifestation. The ancient Hawaiians were simple seed-planters and knew that anything could be brought into reality by observing certain laws of the Universe having to do with the care and tending of the seed.

George: What are the most important differences between the ancient wisdom of *huna* and Western medicine?

Pila: The difference between night and day. Rediscovery of the old truths from a premise of light and wholeness existing in and back of all things will prove Western medicine to be as crude as meat carving or auto mechanics.

George: Do you think it possible for a Westerner to learn the Hawaiian way of healing?

Pila: The children, no problem. We are living in an age of miracles and anything is possible including penetrating the density of that iron fortress called the educated Western mind. Symbolically this is what is unfolding now on our planet. Western thought has come full circle to embrace Eastern thought. The male, left-brained Western knowledge balancing with the female right-brained Eastern wisdom. Metaphorically and physically this is why the Big Island of Hawaii is so important. It is the most isolated place on Earth and a stage setting for the first working model of this symbiosis. As I say in my books on Hawaii:

"In the middle of the ocean where East meets West is the Island of Fire and Ice, home of the volcano and doorway to another dimension and a different reality. Here magic lives, where the Earth itself liquefies and nothing is quite as it seems."

❀ Thirteen

The Way Home

Kapu System:
The Great Polynesian Coverup

It is a popular belief that the islands of Hawaii were discovered and settled by Polynesians in recent history. The story goes that when the Great White ghost *Pa'ao* stormed the beaches of Hawaii in 750 A.D. or thereabouts (some say 1250 A.D.,) he slaughtered the gentle people, using them for fish bait, there beginning the order of *Ku,* the warrior God. The question is, if they were the first, then who were the gentle people that were defeated? Recently decoded chants from the Island of *Moloka'i* say their ancestors were never defeated and were there for thousands of years prior.

They speak of a time before the *Ku* aspect was exiled when there were three tribes, or aspects. *Lono* was the intellectual aspect which always argued with *Ku.* Both were held in abeyance (instead of polarity) by the third, intrinsic factor of the Trinity known in some chants as *Kane,* a term misunderstood because of its modern day association with the male sex.

Many of the American Indian tribes have similar legends to my tribe, telling of where we all originated from on this planet before the fall from grace—a place of indescribable beauty and lushness, with no winter, surrounded by endless water—a place called the Garden.

Before man's horrible inhumanity to man, before unspeakable acts were perpetrated by the *lost children* who were banished to *kahiki* (oblivion, the place beyond the Garden, beyond the horizon) there existed one rule to live by, known as *Aloha mai ke Akua ipo:* "to love yourself as you love God." It was truly a Golden Rule. To live it was simple: The full understanding of it was simple: "Whatever I do to you, I do to myself."

Being children of self-worth, without fear or guilt, this rule was never broken because all of the Children of the Rainbow knew that the responsibility of their own acts came from within and their own personal connection to God. Knowing that they were formed in the likeness and image of the one true God Almighty, they needed only three guidelines (again the trinity) so that they could view the one Golden Rule more objectively, from three angles. The three angles formed a single triangle, all angles leading back to the One rule.

One angle, *kalana* had to do with accuracy of living. It was the rule called *Hala* which today means to sin. Like the word sin it is misunderstood. Sin comes from the Latin, a term used in ancient archery which means to miss the target. *Hala* actually means to stray away from the fragrance or the essence of life. The only punishment for sin was to aim again until you hit the target. *Hala* is also the name for a tree with many sharp branches leading away from its trunk with its roots above the ground. A tree split into male and female where only the male carries the fragrant blossoms capable of pollination, often out of reach to continue propagation.

The second angle on the Golden Rule had to do with balance. It was called *Hewa* which today is known as going overboard, or doing something excessively. To become too fat or starve yourself were issues of *Hewa,* or to take too much (greed) or not enough of something (denial) were violations of *Hewa.* The punishment was ridicule because the violations were considered silly. Ridicule was used to balance because the offender needed outside influence to rectify his own balance. The loss of balance stemmed from seeing things from the narrow vision that comes from being too much into one's own way of doing things. *Hewa* really means to find the interval, the space between waves or sounds—the pulse, the eye of the storm. To properly observe *Hewa* can be applied in everything from surfing a wave to eating a proper meal, to regulating the sound on your boom box so the neighbors don't scream . . . causing *them* to violate *Hewa.*

The third angle or attitude towards living in harmony had to do with understanding the flow of energy. It was called *'Ino,* which today means wicked or vicious. Some say that it originally meant "to intentionally do harm to another with hate in mind" which was the worst unpardonable sin in Paradise, in which the offender was expelled from the community. Even this has a deeper meaning because originally there were no negative words in Paradise. Everything had a positive understandable meaning. The negative connotation for *'Ino* means stormy, simply meaning energy piled up upon itself which can cause a short-circuit or explosion. Fundamentally it has to do with handling power and the abuse of it. *'Ino* actually means to intensify the source within or fully express oneself. The worst abuse (which was unheard of for centuries in Paradise) was rape or murder. Both victim and perpetrator were held responsible for not understanding *'Ino*. If the victim died they were still contacted through the living ancestry because death was not considered a real thing. The clarification and sorting out of the abuse was still possible and forgivable and could only be done by looking within and accepting full responsibility for what had happened.

These were the only original rules in Paradise. There were no "don'ts" because any subject that was forbidden became the feeding ground for negativity. In other words, to even think about, focus on or give homage to things that you didn't want would, sooner or later, cause those very things to creep into your world. Rules were only structured around the good things that you did want. The bad things dissolved from lack of attention. There is a saying in Paradise from *huna,* made popular by Serge King: "Energy flows where attention goes." Where it ceases to go, things whither.

Finding the Way Home

The way out of our madness and finding our way in the midst of the confusion of broken rules and a legal system that no longer works is simple, as is all the wisdom of the original teaching. Begin with yourself and your children by describing what you do want, not what you don't want to happen. Discipline them only with what you want done, not what they did wrong. This is not a form of denying or ignoring bad things. It is a way of seeing through mistake and mishap and clarifying your own truth about them. Try this at home and you will transform yourself and your family. Try this at work and you will begin to transform all the rules of law and business for yourself. Instead of signing 100 pages of loopholes and things that can go wrong, trumped up by lawyers who will be the only ones who get fat from it, try this with your next business contract. Draw up your next lease or partnership agreement on one page, based only upon what you want to happen and do together. If you find a partner willing to grapple and overcome his fear of what can go wrong and relinquish his need for lawyer protection, and if he is another human interested in the joy of succeeding and the willingness to trust, then you have both found your way home to Paradise and out of the insanity. If you are forced to still sign the 100 pages of "don'ts and things to go wrong" then keep this one page also. Bring it out and dust it off whenever there is argument and you will be surprised which one holds up.

Focusing on the good intent can lift you out of the growing insanity of a culture full of people lost in becoming like rodents over the spoils of rules that no longer work. The next thing you know you will be doing business with the honesty and morality of the handshake that built a nation, despite all the thieving and killing that was going on during that time of great change. Next you will no longer have need of courtrooms or lawyers because you have focused on, and have begun to know, your own intent and what to expect of life, instead of succumbing to the confusion of fancy words that only skilled rodents have grown to know the meaning of.

This new-found competence and natural ensuing sense of well-being could spread into your health and further well-being, no longer requiring the skilled cutting of the medical profession—the portion of healers who became focused upon the search for disease. Many of them, just in the last few years, have already joined you on the path of clarification. MDs have begun to study nutrition and are focusing on holistic healing, the power of the body, instead of the mechanics of the body.

Indeed, by stripping away all the rules and getting back to the simple basics of focusing on the fun and joy of what you want, you may (even in the midst of a seeming holocaust) find yourself back in the Garden, not necessarily the one that the world knows as Paradise (although you should visit to remind and refresh yourself) but the Garden of Paradise described by the Children of the Rainbow as the place within and the connection to God.

Legends of the Gentle Stewards
The Legend of the High Order

"When time comes full circle, whether it be in a thousand years or a hundred centuries, the Old Ones of the High Order will return. In a wave of false prophets they go unrecognized, for they are the prophecy. They are not the shouters. In service of humanity they quietly do what needs to be done."

In the moment of the dark hour when the wars of *Ku* and rumors of wars of *Lono* are at their saturation they rise, not in rebellion. Their conch sounds, a distant song of the soul as gentle as a mother to her child. Their light shines forth piercing the hopelessness and insanity. They walk in the opposite direction. Their call falls not on the deaf ears of the multitudes for they be lost in the games of a world half gone mad. Follow their guidance but know your own, for they know the way home, back to the sanity, back to the love, back to the Garden—back to Paradise.

The Return of the Light Warrior
The Tribal Connection: Peoples of the Earth

The most significant of my discoveries in *huna* are the striking similarities of the teaching of my tribe, the Cherokee, with that of other indigenous tribes.

Powwows with a deep connection to North American, Alaskan and Canadian Indians significantly began on the Big

Island of Hawaii in 1985. After teaching their chiefs and medicine men *huna* they have all responded in unison with, "What you have taught us is what our elders speak of as the old ways."

It is now my opinion that all tribal peoples, that is, all peoples of the Earth who did not aspire technologically, share the same wisdom. I refer to it in Hawaiian as "the First People, the First Teaching"—a wisdom beyond anything embraced in popular metaphysics and the other Caucasian paths of enlightenment.

It is my prediction that a missing piece, isolated in the outer islands connected with Aboriginal Dreamtime and the Maori people, will return to the Hawaiian Islands, reactivating this very powerful knowledge to its full potency. Pieces of this puzzle can also be found in Hopi legend. It will happen soon. I believe it is the explanation for the phenomenal gathering of healers and teachers on the Big Island and other key vortexes of energy that began significantly in the early 1980s.

> *"And 144 thousand Light Warriors with their shields balanced, male and female, respecting all paths as one, will return to help the Planet in her time of need."*

> —Hopi Legend

The Return of Shamanism

In times of great change the power shifts from all things big and goes back to the small. The power waivers in that which has become conglomerated, that which was built upon the old. Power reverts back to the individual. All truth can then only be found with the individual. Such it is in this time of greatest change in all history.

To maintain sanity, the first job for us as individuals is to re-identify ourselves. In this process we welcome back the returning shaman. The shaman's path brings back the simple and unadorned way, a direction of pure joy and excitement, the way of the adventurer, not the warrior.

The first evolvement of the shamanistic nature is in learning to weave your way through life by rising above conflict. The shaman learns to observe life, never polarizing energy and getting over the need to take issue. To gain shamanic Mastery is to realize that all that happens is a manifestation of your own awareness. To accept full responsibility for your life is to gain command. With the shaman there is no victim-consciousness. When there is no victim there is no ground for negativity to breed upon. Then the time of greatest upset may become the time of adventure and opportunity. Shaman are incognito. More and more can be found in the workplace. They have even been known to wear suits and ties, and especially dresses.

The Child Holds a Key

The eyes of a child hold a trust that is the unquestioned support of God. This is the innocence that explores the world in child-like wonderment, in the fun of a game, not warring but adventuring, bringing back the joy which is the pure excitement of living in our Maker's creation. It is no wonder that the original Stewards of the Garden called themselves "The Children of the Rainbow." What we must remember is that the innocence of the child holds the only protection, a connection that is our God-Link. Dare to be vulnerable. Heal and embrace the inner child. Lift him from disillusionment, no matter what he has been through. Allow him to once again come out and play . . . for all he is worth. That worth is the only true worth.

This is the message of all tribal peoples, those who have

remained out of their heads and close to their hearts and the Earth Mother. Those who would pierce the membrane of their anger and grief and bring back the missing piece that is their heritage and stewardship as God's children of the Earth. They are the gentle stewards who must fly the banner of their heritage for all the human race, even though they have suffered the loss of everything. Everything except that which can never be destroyed.

Their connection with Great Spirit can only be found through the mother side of our knowing, the intuitive side, the surrender side. It brings back the only thing that will heal a planet in her time of need; the thing that is the love called *aloha*. There is an old Hawaiian saying, "There are no adults, only kids." The young ones that know how to play and love life and the old wrinkled ones who sometimes forgot how. There would be no overblown egos, no power-hungry monsters, no cult-masters and no warmongers . . . if we all remembered that we're just God's little brats.

PART IV

Echoes from an Ancient Future

"The distant conch has sounded and there are those who know and have begun to walk with courage in the other direction— a courage beyond armor which comes only from reconnecting to the trust in the force that animates all hearts—a courage that leads out of confusion towards the light and back to joy."

❀ Fourteen

Hawaii –
The Call Home

The gathering began to take form in 1986 or thereabouts. One by one, they began to come to this island, the Island of Fire. Without a conscious reason or any fanfare, they came. On the other islands, the New Age ruckus was in full swing. Gurus and their open-mouthed and glassy-eyed followers channeled every saint including Bernard, some wisdom, some drivel and a lot of hoopla. Mostly, it served to alienate and polarize the fundamental Christian community.

Meanwhile, on the Big Island, the island of transformation and new beginnings, others were returning home, some to stay, most to simply connect and make sense of their destinies. Some were old warriors with deep battle scars of life. Some came with dignity and knowing, some had been pronounced terminally ill. Others just washed up on the beach, not really knowing why. They all had a common story:

211

"I don't really know what I'm doing here, I just had to come." Or, "Something called me," and "What is it—what is this feeling I get here—on this island, the strangeness, yet somehow familiar?"

Legend says it is Pele's job to bring the emotions to the surface. Many of us who live here and have gone through all the melodrama that life can hold, fondly call it "the dirty laundry island." We say that you cannot stand barefoot on Pele's *pahoehoe* (smooth lava) without the things you need to resolve bubbling to the surface. Some have encountered their souls in the process and have recognized their destiny.

Since the 1980s, it has been my honor to welcome over 140 of these magnificent souls whom I feel may change the direction of our planet. Their initiation at the Place of Refuge was a distant conch heard only by them. One by one thousands of others have made their own personal connection to this place we call the Edge of Eternity, *Pu'u Honua O'Honaunau.*

The similarities in the stories are astonishing. Many have had "near death" experiences. Many share my vision from Vietnam, including the strange buildings to be built for healing centers, alternative medicine and a new kind of university for transcendent thought and ancient studies. Things and a vision that we hope will help a world in its time of need.

Returning to the Earth:
The New Human

I have said that in a time of great change it becomes paramount to survival to re-identify the individual and clarify the belief system. The indigenous peoples of the Earth and their tribal wisdom hold a key for us all to help us through the next phase of change. This wisdom is nurturing and grounding to the individual psyche providing a stronger foundation for all healthy belief systems.

The peoples of the Earth are discovering that the essence beneath their conflicting beliefs is the same. It is the Earth connection that honors all paths as leading toward the one. Perhaps this is the "rock" that is spoken of in scripture, upon which to build one's "church." A touch of this wisdom will enhance the lifestyle, providing balance and comfort for the long road ahead. Comfort for the roller-coaster ride that has already begun.

Along with physical exercise, enhance your life with some form of centered meditative technique. Hawaiians find that the easiest way to meditate is to contemplate. Since it is humanly impossible to empty the mind of thought, just think of what gives you joy. Next thing you know your thoughts are focused and your body is happy. It only takes a few minutes a day. This can be as simple as quiet music and, if you like, a stick of incense to clear the air. This alone will have an immediate effect on the mental stress that is one of the modern-day plagues. Many have totally eliminated their migraine headaches in a few short days by following this practice.

Simple ritual is another great tool to sharpen the focus of your everyday experiences. Your unconscious is the doorway to your greatness and your higher connection and it loves ritual. Hawaiians were masters of ritual, realizing that the power is not in ritual, but in helping you focus to tap into your own power. You may be unaware of the many rituals that you already perform each day. It is easy to put these lost moments to work for you at a higher level of understanding. Whenever you are in the shower, perform the cleansing ritual. It goes like this. The question to your unconscious is: "What needs cleaning up in my life?" The affirmation to perform the ritual is: "As I scrub my body I cleanse my thoughts and my world." The physical performance is a powerful suggestion in unlocking the further power of your mind. The unconscious easily focuses and gets the point by simply considering these notions. What needs eliminating from your life? Think of it when you are on the "porcelain throne" in the morning. You will be surprised at how fulfilling it is to get rid of things symbolically that have troubled you as your body performs its morning constitutional. Brushing your teeth? What is it that you need to get your teeth into for direction and control in your life.

A simple contemplation while performing mechanical tasks will heighten everything from the effectiveness of your food intake to your prosperity and goal-consciousness. The power of blessing food has lost its significance for most people. Here is the simple ritual. Take a moment and be thoughtful before eating. Think of what it took to grow the food and get it to your table. Acknowledging and blessing your meal lifts it out of the category of common organic matter into a magical feast of love and care for the nourishment of your body, mind and spirit. The Hawaiians say that this eliminates all contaminants and reactivates the intrinsic factor of the food. Next thing you know it tastes better, and who knows, perhaps it nourishes better. After all, the part of you that loves ritual, your *unihipili,* your unconscious, knows how to feed each cell and eliminate what you no longer need, with each breath.

There is a saying in Paradise that if it works it is *huna.*

The single most important factor of *huna* and tribal wisdom is the common connection to the Earth Mother. The roots of all these teachings most assuredly share the same goddess paradigm. This comes with a profound love and respect for all life which is healthy for any psyche. It is also a great legacy to give your kids.

No matter what your racial or ethnic background you can experience transformations in practicing these simple principles. We are entering into a new dimension of seeing and feeling and must be more sensitive to our surroundings. This requires psychic development to maintain sanity. We are living in a time where what you see is not necessarily what is really going on beneath the surface. The tribal wisdom of *huna* naturally develops psychic ability through simple languaging with the unconscious and a sensitive "Earth connection" to the environment. The Hawaiian premise for living is that everything is alive. Now we know that we are all made of the same atomic stuff. There is a little story from the *huna* of one of our great departed *kahunas,* Morna Simione, that will illustrate this Hawaiian viewpoint and help you immediately tap into your psychic abilities.

She tells of a student who decided to talk with his shoes. Now that seems silly, doesn't it? Well, the notion crossed his mind one day as he started to put his shoes in the closet. Hawaiians always take their shoes off when they come home. It had been a particularly hard day and perhaps he was tired, but the thought crossed his mind that his shoes didn't want to go into that old dark closet. Funny thought, huh? So, they seemed to say (or so he thought they said), "We think we would like to go out on the porch today." He asked why, looking over his shoulder and feeling silly about the imaginary conversation. The answer? "Because it is nice and sunny out there and we can air out and enjoy the sunshine!" Made sense to him, so he humored his shoes. This went on for a week until one day the shoes said no. "We want to stay in the closet today." Startled, the student asked why. The shoes said, "Because it is going to rain." . . . And it did.

The Veil Has Lifted

The membrane that separates our meager three-dimensional reality from the infinite has always been torn in sacred places. Places connected to star alignments. Places like the Bermuda Triangle and places where the Earth itself liquefies. Here, in the islands of Paradise, the veil is thinnest, a celestial alignment from the end of eternity, softening the dense mundane world, dissolving it into infinite realities. Now that the veil of centuries is lifting, certain things may no longer be true.

For Humankind nothing is more painful than to live in a truth that is no longer. Man (woman) is the only creature who is naked in nature. He clothes himself in his myths of God. This is the only way he can make sense of his world. The problem comes in finding that things are not what they seem. It challenges the validity of all our truths. Man has always had a feeling that there is a greater reality. That feeling is the *ano ilai lo ho i,* his seedling of light. What we are going through that looks like a collapse of society is actually the clarification of our truth. I have said that during a time of great change all power shifts from the built up, the conglomerated, the big, back to the small, the individual. You have the only power now. It comes from listening inside. The gurus of Eastern philosophy call it the still small voice within. What you need to remember is that the answers are not outside. No matter what you have come to believe about yourself or what you have been through, you have the connections to the Universe within you. You are wired that way from God's factory. It all has to do with coming to know your self-worth. Through knowing your own self-worth comes the memory of who you really are and who you were formed in the likeness of. The *Children of the Rainbow* want to share these secrets with you and more. The gentle stewards of Paradise have been waiting for centuries to welcome their lost brothers and sisters home again. In the midst of confusion and a crazy world, can you hear the distant conch?

Return to Paradise by stripping away all that stands in the way, all the buildup, the complication and confusion. Ask of yourself, as the clock speeds up, as the horse runs wild, as the train derails, the planes crash and the bombs go off. Ask yourself, as the precious moments of your life fly by, "What really counts?" Dare to claim back the sacred ground of you and the love of family. Start living the simplicity that is the singular Golden Rule: Do unto others as you would have them do unto you.

The Unraveling of Time

A year has become a month which is now a week on the planet. Such is the illusion that we call time as the saturation of an age is reached. Change your clocks in this manner and it will help you, for your time on the earthly plane is gone in the twinkling of an eye. It will help you hold life precious, for the time of greatest change can be the time of greatest miracles. Walls that would take centuries to dismantle are coming down overnight and this is only the beginning. Breakthroughs are so instantaneous that they are obsolete before press-time.

There are people living now who have witnessed over 90 percent of all that has ever manifested on the earthly realm, and you haven't seen anything yet.

Here on the Island of Fire and Ice, the crossroads of space-time continuum, it is even more intense. Here, with thought and attitude, doorways may be passed through, bridging the thresholds of other realities.

All of the colors come together in the tapestry of life, here where solid becomes liquid. Here one can see from the high mountain and begin to realize that all life is but a single painting. A single tapestry, even though there be thousands of threads going in all directions. One painting, even though the colors are infinite.

At the saturation point of the old, before the new is recognized, there is the stage of transition. While the caterpillar

agonizes in confusion there is a place within of new formation. It is a stage setting, a special place, neither belonging
to the old nor the new. A doorway, where the new creature
can first see the mirror of himself and what is to be. Here,
metaphorically where all roads cross, at the edge of eternity
is that special place, the place within the Earth Mother, the
cocoon for all humanity. The place that all the world calls
Paradise and our Crown Mystery . . . Hawaii.

The Secret Ceremonies

In October of 1989, one of several secret meetings took
place on the Big Island of Hawaii. It was my deep honor to
participate in this gathering.

It is said that such meetings have not taken place in over
2,000 years. They took place near South Point, the southernmost tip of the United States and the rip in the veil. Within
a specific energy grid, a quiet ritual was conducted at this
vortex of unexplained phenomena. The time and celestial
alignment were exact determining factors.

At that time, the following energies were *removed permanently* from the earthly field. This has caused and will
cause these issues to rapidly surface and come to an explo-
sive head. Removed was the breeding ground for:

- Individual power in government
- Greed in general, especially the fast-buck syndrome in
  economics
- Outdated conclusions in education
- Mystery, guilt and fear in religion
- Mystery and chemical use in medicine
- Perversion and tricks in law
- Science for science's sake without moral responsibility
- Distorted patterns and sounds in music and art
- Sex without love

- Everything but the God-that-you-are in the self-image

Those of the Celestial Family also declared that the only further importance of possessions would be for service, not for personal gain. Removing bullshit from politics was also attempted, but it was found that some things couldn't be accomplished, even by the Higher Forces in the known Universe.

Evolution and disintegration will naturally speed up in all the aforementioned areas.

Whether or not it actually happened, there is an interesting set of coincidental circumstances unfolding. Explore this for yourself. Institutions may begin to act as though there is no "hook to hang the issues on" anymore. Wouldn't that be nice? Who knows—it might have affected world communism and helped bring a few walls down.

The next meeting of this sort was conducted under similar circumstances in Kona on the Big Island, January 16, 1992. It was declared that the present emotional and mental bondage "aura" of the planet must be broken up and dissolved. Along with it shall go:

- Processed (contained) fear
- Mystery in general
- Guilt in general
- Industrial greed and power
- Past conclusions of tricks and perversions

As the illusion of time is speeded up, which is an effect of the evolutionary threshold, certain events will continue to happen in extreme form. On the positive side are the mysteries being revealed, with incredible breakthroughs in all fields of endeavor. On the negative side, depending on how you are connected with it, even more rapid disintegration can be expected, with focus upon the exposing of corruption.

These issues may still appear to exist but their foundation is crumbling.

New Age hocus-pocus? Actually old age, indeed ancient age. As the mysteries are revealed, we will find that most of what we have chosen to believe is a left-brained coverup called "his story." All of this is found in an original tribal wisdom shared with all the peoples who remained close to the Earth.

The roots of this wisdom that I have discovered in ancient Hawaiian *huna* are said to be passed down for 812 generations. This is a mind-boggling 26,000 years. Aboriginal Dreamtime parallels this, dating back 30,000 years.

This information is contained in chants from the island of *Moloka'i* never before interpreted into English. I have found the chant to be much more accurate than the written word, revealing actual "essence" and an in-depth sensory impression of what really took place.

Having shared much of this information with the elders and shamans of many North American Indian tribes, we have determined that the teaching is the same. This commonality of wisdom appears with the Maori and other tribal cultures as well.

A new look at the Hawaiian chant of Origin, the *Kumulipo,* is revealing a startling new understanding of creation seen clearly only through the eyes of quantum physics. This substantiates some Biblical scripture as never before and could expose other scripture as half-truths.

The misunderstood Mayan/Hopi event of 1987, popularly called the Harmonic Convergence, was the platform for these specific shifts in universal consciousness that are now occurring. Since that event even the uninitiated should now realize that something is up.

 # Fifteen

The Symptoms
of *Aloha*
or Inner Peace

At first the returning shaman may go unnoticed in the crowd. They seem to be passive but a more accurate description is "non-explosive." It is because they have become infected.

Aloha is most recognizable in the eyes and sometimes in the demeanor. I must warn you that, if you travel to Hawaii, it is highly contagious, but only if your defenses are down. If you are one of those who has become weary of life's battles, you are vulnerable to infection.

If you are vulnerable to change, watch out for a total transformation to occur. Don't worry about embarrassment. You won't go around babbling scripture and trying to save souls. Those are the symptoms of fear of losing what you finally found.

If you are wondering if you have been infected by "it," I now have the diagnosis and symptomology. Early signs like braying at the moon over Hawaiian songs and crying at the *hula,* or getting gooseflesh over the chant are common. You've been exposed, but still may not be infected. That could still pass one day, on the freeway under the drone of a car radio.

If you have truly contracted the disorder, it will affect your whole life and things will never be the same. Thanks to fellow travelers Mr. and Mrs. Jeff Rockwell, here are the real symptoms:

1. A tendency to think and act spontaneously, rather than from fears based upon past experiences.
2. An unmistakable ability to enjoy each moment.
3. A loss of interest in conflict.
4. A loss of interest in judging others.
5. A loss of conflict.
6. A loss of interest in interpreting the actions of others.
7. A loss of ability to worry (this is a very serious symptom).
8. Frequent, overwhelming episodes of appreciation.
9. Content feelings of connection with others and nature.
10. Frequent attacks of smiling through the eyes of the heart (a dead giveaway for a carrier).
11. Increasing susceptibility to love extended by others as well as the uncontrollable urge to extend it.
12. An increasing tendency to let things happen

rather than to make them happen. (At this stage the disorder is untreatable.)

Although it is contagious only to those who surrender to it, the disorder is nevertheless serious and, although never terminal, it may lead to further consequences and seemingly unacceptable behavior. The advanced stages may have to do with the equator or the humidity in the tropics. In the islands there has been observed the following additional symptomology:

1. Laughing out of context, from the gut, often shaking the windows.
2. Tears of joy over the littlest of things.
3. A totally calm response when all hell is breaking loose.
4. No further interest in "victim consciousness."
5. Yawning through the 6 o'clock news.
6. Turning off the 6 o'clock news.
7. Other inappropriate responses, such as a sigh of relief when someone says the world is coming to an end.
8. Your neighbor buys a gun just as you decide to start hugging strangers.
9. Talking to trees.
10. Delusions of grandeur and a sense of being guided.
11. An unexplained sense of well-being and feeling that all is in order. (Watch it. They can lock you up for this one.)
12. Some have been found standing in line at the Savings & Loan demanding back their Trust. Others have been caught dropping their insurance.

13. Retiring from work permanently, rolling up
    your sleeves and getting on with the full-time
    job of serious play.

Remember, institutions are filled with these symptoms. Most of the above is considered unacceptable behavior in a falling society.

As the disorder spreads into charisma and your mystique increases, others will begin sticking to you like magnets. Warn them of infection when they begin coming to you for a "fix" and asking for answers to questions to which you do not have a clue.

The disorder can be lonely at times. While others are growing old, you will have drifted in the opposite direction. Preoccupied with their problems, the masses will have less and less time for you.

It can be taxing, too. Except for those infected, others come around only in times of crisis and only when they want something, which seems to be more and more often.

If you have found yourself on this long path to recovery, cheer up. You will meet others and we can always pray for an epidemic. Many have come to us for inoculation since our infection. A strange side-effect has been observed in some people leaving their terminally ill symptoms behind.

Many times it all started with a joke I shared with them when they had taken life too seriously. It was given to me by Da Da Ghi, a holy man from India. I think he was once a Hawaiian. He said that if you have lost the business, your house and your wife, after you have been pronounced terminally ill and life has dealt you the worst blows, there is only one duty left. That duty is to crawl, if you have to, over to the nearest mirror, hoist yourself up, look deeply into it and with your last breath, say aloud seven times . . .

"Cock-a-doodle-do!!!"

Through the years I have gotten many strange phone calls, sometimes in the wee hours of the morning. Rarely leaving their names, these callers will say, "Pila, is that you?" I will say, "Yes." They will say, "Cock-a-doodle-do" and hang up.

I know then that another friend along the way has seen through the illusion. Another shaman is receiving his enlightenment. It was years before I realized the simple Hawaiian wisdom of this humor. I had thought it was a vent for hysteria but "cock-a-doodle-doo" is the rooster acknowledging the light of a new day . . . a new beginning.

Sixteen

Every Island Has Its Magic

This work is focused mainly on the Big Island, Hawaii; however, anyone who travels elsewhere and wishes for a deeper connection to the Islands of Paradise may find it worthy of a read. Worthy, that is, *if* you can take a few meditative moments in your venture (poolside or at the beach in Oahu, Mau'i, Kaua'i, or elsewhere) and make the effort to penetrate the white-noise static, "traffic-jamb" cloud that is traditional tourism. My "Island Chakra Journey" (found on page 52, or the recorded version with music, which can be found at www.qdreams.com/index. php?cPath=3) will begin to explain special energies unique to each island that you can get in touch with. *The Secrets & Mysteries of Hawaii* was inducted into the International Theosophical Society research archive in

2004, along with the new interpretation of the Dead Sea scrolls. The concepts and interpretations also align with continuous new findings in quantum physics and its "languaging and interpretation" . . . which is proving to be pure *kahuna* viewpoint. Not only is the Ancient Hawaiian description of human mind function healthier than the Carl Jung three aspects of self and any current concept in modern psychology, it is more accurate as well.

Oahu, "The Gathering Place," is the island vital to discovering ones "supreme individuality." *When making this earnest connection, the island also gives focus and direction to those souls seeking it.* Some of the important "power points" of such (that are convenient):

The Duke's statue on Waikiki Beach is your first easy connection. Millions of young people worldwide are already intuitively connecting there yearly for this purpose (whether conscious or not). And what is more supremely and individually empowering than surfing!? Duke "Paoa Kahinu Mokoe Hulikohola" Kahanamoku is the recognized Herculean demigod of the art and skill, at least in our hemisphere. Aussies may have their own. It is important to note that Henry Ford didn't invent the automobile, just made it "viable." It is also important to note that inventions, even the airplane, "phenomenally happen" *simultaneously* around the world. To paraphrase Victor Hugo: "Nothing can stop the idea whose time has come." To any seeker evolved beyond Keith Bennett's "chaos theory of evolution," this fact alone is *proof* of higher design, better understood in the Ancient Hawaiian Wisdom axiom "Dreams, the source of all reality."

The power point that is the island of *Oahu* is another connection. One is more likely to *feel* the connection of one's "blossoming supreme individuality" on a core-level

while surfing anywhere on the island. Surfing (and perhaps flying a plane or conquering Everest) could be considered individuality's "metaphor" (symbolic essence).
The color spectrum blue will help this focus, especially
lighter blues and turquoise. Leaving a lei offering at the
Duke statue may commemorate this focus and intent.
Allow the demigod Duke to be your teacher, friend,
brother, and guide. Few realize that he was given the
respect among *kahunas* as the highest of priests.

Duke was a man of few words in his early days. *He*
knew what was in his bright mind, but trying to communicate it for him was like talking to an alien.
Therefore, he swam and surfed in solitude from dawn to
dusk, as the stories go. Modern legend says that the other
kahunas ridiculed him as "the one who did nothing but
play all day long." Then one day, he was challenged by
the most sophisticated of healing *kahunas,* the Lapa'au,
who said, "We know all the herbs, their intricacies, and
myriad applications. What do you know?" "Some things
you don't," replied the Duke, the man of few words.
"Even things the *kahuna* Pu'ali and Kīpu'upu'u (martial
artists) don't know. The so-called learned ones perked
their ears! "For all mastery of life can be learned in the
wave," continued the Duke of men. "Life is like a wave.
If you are arrogant and try to control, it will crush you.
If you are too late, too lazy, and do not hear its call, you
will suffer a worse fate still, that of being left behind. *But,*
the one who learns to ride the wave in balanced bliss
experiences the power and exaltation known only to the
gods."

The Wizard Bell Stones: A second questionable power
point you may or may not wish to connect with is con-
veniently located just east of the Duke's statue. The monument is known also as the Wizard Healing Stones or

"Bell Rocks." They too have a mysterious story and contain magic, and they were originally used for healing; specifically for purging the body's entire energy field, balancing, and thereby significantly strengthening the immune system against most disease and disorder. The problem I have with this is that a young girl was sacrificed to seal the deal. I don't know that her bones still lie at the base but suspect so. The stones were brought forth by priests with a visionary mission to amend earlier acts of Pa'ao, the Polynesian warrior who originally conquered the Hawaiian Islands. These priests returned to Hawaii from the outpost Society Islands (collectively known as "Tahiti"). Desiring to go home after years of healing in Hawaii, they spent a month in ritual, transferring their spiritual healing power (mana, mana) to the stones.

People needing healing and students from around the world including traditional medicine practitioners, have connected with these stones. The ritual of connection has to do with walking clockwise around the stone cluster while "asking" in the name of aloha (and hopefully the poor girl sacrifice) for your healing or for the healing of a loved one. To remotely send this energy (if you are okay with this), simply visualize the people in need with smiles upon their faces . . . while sending your aka (silvery cord) or rainbow connection. This simple notion is a most powerful missing link to most forms of prayer and meditation. (Then you might want to try washing your thoughts of the human sacrifice involved!) As for the possible witchcraft aspects, what was magic is now being revealed as science. Hitler, unfortunately, was our first modern proof of that fact. And he wasn't the first to fiddle with the lid of Pandora's box. It's now all about quantum physics. I believe the ancient Hawaiians to be the first "quantum physicians." The magic works for anyone, and I have the same concerns over human sacrifice with some dreaded monument restorations on the Big Island. Hawaiians need to realize what they are doing in the name of sovereignty and Lono! (Polynesian anger is not original Hawaiian Wisdom, it is the cover-up . . . the Kapu System that cost them everything!)

Pali Lookout: If you are in a transition and need to re-access, the Pali Lookout is a wonderful metaphor for this. As you look down into the incredibly beautiful windward side of *Oahu,* its island harbors and stunning emerald green mountain chards, reminiscent of the Napali, your ritual here is to say good-bye, in thoughts of sunset (toward the rising of a new day), to all your regrets in life. To do so lovingly is to finally find release. To do so with those things that angered you and you could do nothing about is to discover your own resurrection, your transformation . . . your phoenix within. The splendid air and altitude in the marvelous setting will help give the deepest level of your *unihipili* (your subconscious computer data bank) this "crossroads, turning-point realization." Even tour buses can't dampen this feeling, and if it rains, consider it your sublime cleansing!

Ghost Tours: A popular trend. To get more than your money's worth, use your *Hakalau* (expanded, or "soft" vision). There is more on the subject in Chapters 10 and 11. Some quick, simplified instruction: Whenever you sense the spirits about, take a deep breath, hum on the exhale, allowing your register to drop from high to low (this will settle you quickly into your *na'au,* greater center of knowing (and get you outta yo head-noise, bra!). Then, defocus (easiest way is to look past your object of focus) while observing your peripheral (out of the corners of your eyes). Warning: You betta have your adult diapers on!! Your "soft" vision is direct access to the higher realms and seeing auras.

It is important to note that a little Ancient Hawaiian Wisdom regarding such sites may prove *very empowering, especially to those seeking personal direction.*

The Martial Arts Connection: For those of Japanese, Chinese, or Korean lineage looking to make your deeper connection: consider that there may be a lost key to one of your great wisdoms here in the islands of paradise, a missing piece to your puzzle, isolated, held pure. In the dawn of the Industrial Age, the great martial arts Order of the Samurai was banished to Hawaii. There is reason to suspect that King Kamehameha the Great employed at least some of the techniques in his mighty warrior sect. Roots of this incredible discipline that was a way of life should indeed warrant further research. In doing so, consider the notion that is the conclusion of tribal peoples from around the planet. To paraphrase the realizations of the many tribal chiefs, medicine men (and women) and elders I have shared 'ava with through the years: "Our survival teachings may be but fractured remnants, pieces of the greater puzzle, that is our star connection."

A few brief notes on the other Hawaiian Islands:

Mau'i: All islands of Hawaii are vortexes that have the own power points peculiar to their chakra (rainbow color) "band." They also overlap. In other words, one may get in touch with the energies of the Big Island elsewhere throughout the chain. They are of the same raw substance "directly from the other *side.*" Peculiar to Mau'i: It is the island of sexual energy: creativity *manifest.*

Warning: Getting pregnant on your wedding night is a *much* higher risk factor here! To put this energy to its highest good, "dream your dreams aloud" of manifesting . . . lest the baby that fills the womb of your thoughts become literal! In particular, "ponder the good and practical business of your dream" here. It will most certainly "oil the gears" and begin aligning the "grand tumblers of the lock." This is why business men of the world romp and play here . . . especially at blue print, prospectus, and contract times. When you're contemplating the actual implementation of a new idea, let your thoughts and dreams come back to "Her third eye," Lahaina. Let the demigod lasso your "mighty sun and bring it to earth."

Kaua'i: You must see the Napali if only from the Prince Hotel, Hanalei. The Kalalau "Kahuna Initiation" Trail lies at the end of the road past Hanalei. The Wet and Dry Caves are on your way (another must). Don't explore the wet caves by inflatable, you'll be lost to the underworld! *Don't* throw yourself on large stones in Kaua'i; they may contain spirits! Southern Grand Canyon is your hiking experience for parallel realities, it has to do with military secrets there, and the energy field that produces popping (singing) beach stones.

Molokai'i, Lana'i, and Ni'ihau are just too much to address in this initial work. If you cannot travel to the outer islands, much can be gained from "witnessing" them from afar. *Mau'i* is your best shot at this, or a coastal excursion now that most of the prop planes are no longer. If you have the resource and are spiritually drawn, *Moloka'i* is your church of churches. *Lana'i,* your outdoor connection to the way it was. Please leave *Ni'ihau* to itself, unless you are part of a legal excursion or a licensed researcher with government permission.

Whether your experience in paradise is realized as Waikiki or the rare outer island connection, the message here is to really *connect.* Experience your paradise within, your own solitary Hawaii. Always remember to step away from the crowd now and then, *look* out of the corners of your eyes a little more, and *feel* with all your senses until you find yourself *tasting* your thoughts! From your first vivid, surreal moments in tasting a trade wind, a part of you will know this is possible. *Don't* let it become a longing afterward. Remember, while you're here in the islands the world dreams of, all you have to do to make your deeper connection is to slow down and *savor* a little more.

 Epilogue

"I give you both a blessing and a curse in the same breath . . . to be born in a time of change."
—Confucius

Wherever you connect to the islands that the world knows as Paradise, there is a part of you that will begin to know and remember: This is more than just sand and palm trees and wonderful weather. It is your greater connection to the Human Spirit, the collective part of us that longs for something greater, the part that is more than human, more than conflict, more than wasteful, meaningless madness.

In this time of greatest change in all history, the prime Hawaiian notion to consider is that "we are coming full circle." The future is not new. It does not go in a straight line but unfolds as a spiral. When viewed from above (a different angle) it is a circle. We are coming full circle. There is something strangely familiar as we look at the old from a different angle. The clutter of all that we have invented and called "new" is not new at all. It is simply the residue of atrophied thoughts, thoughts that have become dense and focused.

Is it the end then, or the beginning, you may ask. With a spiral it must go on. With a circle it matters not. To go on, the spiral this time must become the circle. To do so requires an embrace.

From here on for those who resist there shall be the sadness of turmoil. For those who leap leaving all behind there shall be excitement with a degree of insanity. But for those who embrace and listen to the conch from the mountaintop the small quiet voice within, there shall be the healing of an ancient severed connection. The connection to Heaven on Earth.

To those who have begun to listen, welcome home, back to the Paradise within you.

From the Island of Fire and Ice,

Aloha,

—*Pila*

Live a More Joyful,
Worthwhile, and Abundant Life

Code #5690 • Paperback • $14.95

Learn to follow your passions and focus
on active appreciation through anecdotes, insightful musings,
candid stories, and hopeful messages.

Nourish Your Body and Soul
In Today's Stressful World

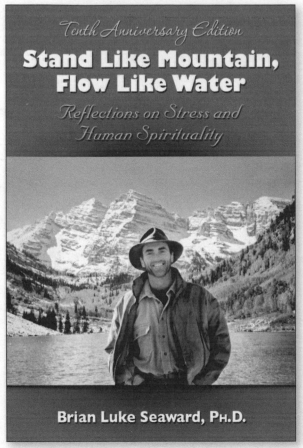

Code #5474 • Paperback • $14.95

Learn to maintain a sense of balance and inner peace.
by embracing the connection between stress
and spirituality.

Enjoy Life

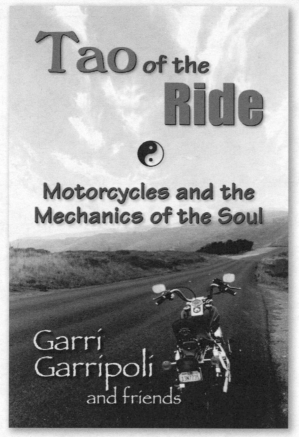

Code #6706 • Paperback • $10.95

Learn how the freedom and exhiliaration of adventure
hold the key to the meaning of life
and the attainment of inner peace.